310 · 478 · 4456
818 · 730 · 9911

AON SERVICES
2 WTC 8.
718-519-0840
718-771-5296
917-803-4964
GREY TOP + BLACK SKIRT

Please Help!!!

CAROL LAPLANTE
212 - 564 - 6512
5'4" White hair

MELENDEZ
ANTONIO
0
B.E. WINDOWS CORP.

MELENDEZ
ANTONIO
B.E. Windows Corp.
WORLD TRADE CENTER

MARIA RAMIREZ
NOW 26 yrs old.
917-251-4404

FRANCISTOR
GERALD 105 Fl.

STACEY SANDERS

WORKPLACE: Marsh. Com. Tower 1 Wtc 96th Floor

DESCRIPTION: 5ft. 6 inches tall, 150 lbs, straight shoulder length brown hair, blue eyes, fair skin, wearing black pants, black sweater, carrying black leather bag.

CONTACT: Martha Sanders at 516-555-7721
Bruno Kaplan at 917-555-0555
Aline Lewis at 917-555-2665

IF YOU HAVE ANY INFORMATION PLEASE CALL

ANGELA SUSAN PEREZ
WORKS FOR CANTOR FITZGERALD
101 ST FL
TOWER

PLEASE CALL WITH INFO:
914. 803. 1040
914. 260. 5446

Antonio Rocha
Company: Cantor Fitzgerald

CONTACT: MARILYN ROCHA 973-889-1719

MISS
KEVIN

NAME: ALISHA LEVIN
EMPLOYER: FUJI BANK
HEIGHT: 5' 5"
WEIGHT: 115 Lbs.
HAIR: BLOND
EYES: BLUE
PLACE OF WORK: TOWER II, WORLD TRADE CENTER

PLEASE CALL (212) 673-54__
ANY INFORMATION ABOUT HER

Looking for:
Scott Hazelcorn
Worked at WTC
at Cantor Fitzgerald
29 Years Old
5'6" 125 lbs.
Scar on 1 leg
Brown Hair
Brown Eyes
Goatee under lip
Call with any information:
1- home - 908-665-2847
2- cell - 908-377-9793
3- work - 212-372-1593
work STC 1511

718-849-5059

Lee
Hoboken

Sean Lugano
Height: 5'9"   Weight: 165
Hair: Brown   Eyes: Brown
Please Call:
212-260-8317
917-407-2545
917-864-2901
917-941-7616
Last Seen: KBW — 88th Floor — Tower 2

Aaron Horwitz
W 14th Street Apt 17D
212-929-1469
Joseph Horwitz (Brother)
212-74-9438
Strawberry birthmark on lip and under nipples
11/15/76 at Beth Israel Hospital
Cantor Fitzgerald
1 World Trade Center
Alan Horwitz (Father)
212-929-1469, 516-810-9266

Passport: Michael Ding
140 E56th Street Apt. 6E
New York, NY 10022
Home 212-558-0745
Email: ding29@hotmail.com

Lee, Yang-Der

HORWITZ

TOR-FITZGERALD

MISSING

Attached is a picture of Jeffrey B. Gardner. He is slender, approx. 5'7" with hazel eyes, brown hair, a mustache and a close cropped beard. He has a tattoo on his outer left ankle of the sun in shades of yellow and gold, a light leddier type birthmark on his ribcage, wears a silver bracelet with blue stones and a gold necklace with a peace symbol on it.

Please call Amy Gardner at 201-963-1969 or 917-439-6892

Please help, we love him and want him back!!!

ERIC L BENNETT
ALLIANCE CONSULTING
1 WTC, 102 fl.
5'11", 184 lbs, Blue eyes, tattoo of bulldog on shoulder

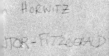

Worked on 102nd Floor of Alliance Consulting Group
Female Caucasian

Jonathan Torgovnik

LIFE

ONE NATION

America Remembers September 11, 2001

LIFE

ONE NATION

America Remembers September 11, 2001

Little, Brown and Company
Boston New York London

LIFE

Editor Robert Sullivan
Creative Director Ian Denning
Picture Editor Barbara Baker Burrows
Senior Editor Robert Andreas
Consulting Editor Richard B. Stolley
Associate Picture Editors Donna F. Aceto, Christina Lieberman
Senior Reporter Hildegard Anderson
Writer/Reporter Loren Mooney
Copy Pam Warren (Chief), Joel Griffiths
Production Manager Michael Roseman
Picture Research Sarah Burrows, Lauren Steel

General Manager Andrew Blau
Finance Director Camille Sanabria

Editorial Operations

Richard K. Prue (Director), Edward G. Carnesi (Manager), Brian Fellows, Stanley E. Moyse, Richard Shaffer (Supervisors), Keith Aurelio, Gregg Baker, Charlotte Coco, Scott Dvorin, Raphael Joa, Rosalie Khan, Po Fung Ng, Barry Pribula, David Spatz, Sara Wasilausky, David Weiner

Published by
Time Warner Trade Publishing

Chairman, Time Warner Trade Publishing
Laurence J. Kirshbaum

Publisher, Little, Brown and Company
Michael Pietsch

Executive Editor
Geoff Shandler

"LIFE" is a registered trademark of Time Inc.

Time Inc. Home Entertainment

President
Rob Gursha

Vice President, Branded Businesses
David Arfine

Executive Director, Marketing Services
Carol Pittard

Director, Retail & Special Sales
Tom Mifsud

Director of Finance
Tricia Griffin

Marketing Director
Kenneth Maehlum

Assistant Director
Ann Marie Ross

Editorial Operations Manager
John Calvano

Associate Book Production Manager
Jonathan Polsky

Associate Product Manager
Jennifer Dowell

Assistant Product Manager
Michelle Kuhr

Special thanks to: Victoria Alfonso, Suzanne DeBenedetto, Robert Dente, Gina Di Meglio, Peter Harper, Roberta Harris, Natalie McCrea, Jessica McGrath, Emily Rabin, Mary Jane Rigoroso, Steven Sandonato, Tara Sheehan, Meredith Shelley, Bozena Szwagulinski, Marina Weinstein, Niki Whelan

A shorter version of this book has been published by Time Inc. Home Entertainment under the title *In the Land of the Free: September 11—And After*.

First Edition

For information on Time Warner Trade Publishing's online publishing program, visit www.ipublish.com

ISBN 0-316-06728-8
Library of Congress Control Number 2001096813

10 9 8 7 6 5 4 3 2

QG

Printed in the United States of America

Joe McNally

Jason Cascone, 22, finished his training on September 10, 2001. The next morning his mother woke him and said there was a fire at the World Trade Center. He remembers being transported to his first assignment with 50 other firefighters: "There was this chaplain on the bus and he was giving absolution to everyone." Please see Faces of Ground Zero, page 142.

Introduction
by Rudolph W. Giuliani

On the morning of September 11, 2001, the United States of America awoke to find itself under attack. In the City of New York, hijacked commercial airliners were crashed into the World Trade Center. Less than two hours later, both 110-story Twin Towers collapsed, killing some 5,000 innocent men, women and children. It was the deadliest day in American history, costing more lives than the attack on Pearl Harbor or D-Day.

In the aftermath of this unimaginable tragedy, New Yorkers, and all Americans, have united as never before. Inspired by countless examples of courage and generosity, we have met the worst of humanity with the best of humanity. The darkest day in our long history has led to our finest hour.

I was having breakfast in midtown when I received word that the first plane had hit the northern tower. It was a clear blue-sky day, but some New Yorkers still held on to the hope that the crash could have been a terrible accident. When the second plane began its deadly descent into the southern tower, we knew that we were under attack.

I arrived at the western base of the World Trade Center to witness the most horrific scene of my life—the buildings were burning, shooting flames and black smoke toward the sky, while debris and human beings fell to the ground. The firefighters and police were already there and the rescue effort was under way. New York's Bravest and New York's Finest were doing what they always do—running toward danger. Among these were the most decorated men in the Fire Department, living legends such as First Deputy Commissioner Bill Feehan,

"We have met the worst of humanity with the best of humanity."

Mark Lennihan/AP

Chief of the Department Pete Ganci, the Department Chaplain Father Mychal Judge, and the rising star of Manhattan's Rescue 1 Squad, Captain Terry Hatton. The best of the Bravest put themselves in the gravest danger. Like many thousands, they would never be seen alive again.

The magnitude of the horror is still hard to comprehend. Those proud Twin Towers that crowned our skyline for a quarter century no longer stand.

Even more devastating is the loss of thousands of individuals who were killed in the attack. All were innocent. All were heroes.

Those who went to work in the World Trade Center on September 11 were engaged in the quiet heroism of supporting their families, pursuing their dreams and playing their own meaningful part in a diverse, dynamic and free society. We will never know many of the selfless acts of courage that occurred among them that day, but they will occupy a sacred place in our hearts and in our history. They will never be forgotten.

The brave men and women who entered the Twin Towers to save those inside are already recognized as heroes for the ages. Survivors of the attack speak of stairwells crowded with people determined to get downstairs to safety, while firefighters, police officers, and other emergency work-

> **The attack was intended to break our spirit. It has utterly failed. Our hearts are broken, but they continue to beat, and the spirit of our City has never been stronger.**

ers were going in the opposite direction—running upstairs toward danger, toward the heart of the fire, determined to save lives. Three hundred forty-three members of the New York City Fire Department lost their lives on September 11—a devastating blow to a Department that had lost 778 men since it was founded in 1865. Members of the New York City Police Department, the Port Authority Police, EMS workers and court officers also made great sacrifices amid startling acts of bravery. Not a single one of those heroes died in vain. Their courage, selflessness and professionalism saved more than 25,000 lives that day—making it the most successful rescue operation in our nation's history. These were true American patriots. They gave their lives in defense of our liberty.

In the last great attack on American soil, the attack on Pearl Harbor, the first casualties were the members of our Navy and other armed services. In this attack, the first uniformed casualties were New York City firefighters, New York City police officers, Port Authority police officers, EMS workers, court officers and other emergency personnel. Their courage and determination should serve as an eternal example to us all. When firefighters run into a burning building, they don't stop to wonder whether the people inside are rich or poor, what race they are, or what religion they practice. Their thoughts are focused solely on the individuals inside that need to be saved. Their actions represent the purest example of love for humanity.

We know that this was not just an attack on the City of New York or the United States of America. It was an attack on the very idea of a free, inclusive and civil society. The victims were of every race, religion and ethnicity, representing 80 differ-

ent nations. Americans are not a single ethnic group. Americans are not of one race or one religion. We are defined as Americans by our belief in political, economic and religious freedom, democracy, the rule of law, and respect for human life.

In some ways, the resilience of life in New York is the ultimate sign of defiance to terrorism. We call ourselves the Capital of the World in large part because we are the most diverse city in the world. Every day, we provide living proof that Christians, Muslims, Jews, Hindus and Buddhists can live side by side and thrive in one city, under one flag, in a spirit of mutual respect. We do not give in to group thinking or group hatred because we know that those are the sicknesses that caused this attack. As a result of our common outrage and suffering, there is a renewed spirit of unity in our City.

This terrorist attack was intended to break our spirit. It has utterly failed. Our hearts are broken, but they continue to beat, and the spirit of our City has never been stronger. On that terrible day, evacuation from lower Manhattan was orderly. Within minutes of the attack, thousands of people lined up outside local hospitals to give blood or help in any way they could. Businesses and individuals made swift donations to aid the rescue effort and the families of the deceased. Groups of people continued to stand along the West Side Highway at every hour of the day and night holding brightly colored handwritten signs encouraging and thanking the rescue workers. On the gray, drizzly Friday that President Bush visited Ground Zero, he inspired exhausted rescue workers with an impromptu speech delivered through a bullhorn handed to him by someone at the site. The instantaneous eruption of cheers reflected the determi-

On the day after, the mayor was back at Ground Zero.

nation of our City and nation.

Now each of us has a responsibility to live our lives with the same courage embraced by those who died in the attacks on the World Trade Center, the Pentagon and the hijacked plane that crashed in Pennsylvania. We have an obligation to honor their memory by doing everything we can to eradicate terrorism, so that no other child is orphaned by its evil. We need to remain united— as individuals, as Americans and as countries committed to life in the civilized world—against the tyranny of terrorism.

As we begin the process of rebuilding our lives and our skyline, we should heed the words of a hymn that I have heard repeatedly at the many memorial services I've attended over the past several weeks: "Be Not Afraid." As Americans, we need to reassert our fundamental human right to live in freedom from fear. Our nation is strong and united, and now more than ever, we are the land of the free and the home of the brave.

Rudolph W. Giuliani

Towering Symbols

They were never meant to be merely buildings.

When the Second World War ended, there was little time to savor victory or to lick wounds, because a new challenge was quickly afoot. It was the cold war, and the free, capitalist system of the United States was threatened by the communism of erstwhile allies in Moscow and Beijing.

It was around this time that discussions began concerning the creation of a world trade facility, a brilliant diadem that would attest to the vitality of America's economic system. For many years, opinions regarding its nature and location defied consensus. In the late 1950s the Port Authority of New York and New Jersey became interested in such a project, and after years more of political infighting, construction began in 1966.

The story of the man chosen to design the World Trade Center is a paradigm of the American dream. Minoru Yamasaki, a second-generation Japanese American who was born into poverty in

Two hundred thousand tons of steel were needed to build the Trade Center. Here, steel assemblies are lifted into place. In order to cope with the incredible heights, cranes that hydraulically boosted themselves were imported from Australia, and thereby dubbed kangaroo cranes.

Frederic Lewis/Hulton Archive

Lambert/Hulton Archive

> **“** I feel this way about it. World trade means world peace and consequently the World Trade Center buildings in New York . . . had a bigger purpose than just to provide room for tenants. The World Trade Center is a living symbol of man's dedication to world peace . . . beyond the compelling need to make this a monument to world peace, the World Trade Center should, because of its importance, become a representation of man's belief in humanity, his need for individual dignity, his beliefs in the cooperation of men, and through cooperation, his ability to find greatness. **”**

> —Minoru Yamasaki, chief architect of the World Trade Center, as the Twin Towers were being built in the early 1970s

Seattle in 1912, worked for 17 cents an hour at a salmon cannery to put himself through the University of Washington. During the Depression, Yamasaki, like many others before and since, took his big ideas to New York, where he landed a job with the firm that designed the Empire State Building, then the tallest in the world. He became known as an artist who wedded attractiveness and func- tional efficiency; he once expressed his aesthetic thusly: "Man needs a serene architectural back- ground to save his sanity in today's world." The Port Authority's commission for the Trade Center— floor space and the like—was clearly defined, and after studying more than a hundred models, Yama- saki settled on seven buildings and a concourse, dominated by the two towers that would, for a

Henry Groskinsky

while, be the highest man-made points on earth.

The last building in the project was completed in 1973. As with anything so prominent, so front-and-center, the World Trade Center was not beloved by all. Some found it too austere; others used terms less polite. Yet many praised the purity of the design, the just-rightness of two huge towers for New York, a city so big they had to name it twice. And the Trade Center drew people to it, not just those who worked there—the center was fully rented out on September 11, 2001—but other New Yorkers, and tourists by the busload. Windows on the World was a perfect setting for dining out in the Big Apple, blending romance with excitement. From the observation deck, on a clear day, you *could* see forever.

Over the years, the World Trade Center, in particular its Twin Towers, grew on the city, winning over many of its detractors. The massive constructs were humanized by a series of events—planned and unplanned—that eventually built a suitably quirky, individualistic Big Apple personality. Frank Sinatra and Liza Minnelli entertained in the nightclubs on high, giving sanction for their crowd, and John Lennon and Mick Jagger visited too, bestowing a different brand of approval. Terrific stunts, widely admired in New York City, were performed

On August 7, 1974, Philippe Petit stretched a cable across the tops of the Twin Towers. Then, as crowds oohed and aahed below, the French daredevil aerialist walked nearly all the way across—and then turned around and went all the way back. New York's Finest were not amused, and arrested the 25-year-old Petit.

America's Security

That vast fortress known as the Pentagon is the embodiment of American will and might, and the building itself, its conception and construction, is a classic example of American can-do. In the summer of 1941, war was pressing toward the U.S. But the offices of the U.S. War Department were scattered across Washington, D.C., in 17 separate locations. A plan was hatched for a mammoth building to house

all sectors of the military. Soon, engineers were working from designs by 400 architects. The site, across the Potomac in Arlington, Va., was a wasteland of swamps and dumps called Hell's Bottom. The five-sided shape, echoing that of fortresses through the centuries, came about partly to conform with the land and also to conserve strategic elements. To minimize the use of steel, stairs and ramps were installed rather than elevators; finally, enough of the vital material was saved to build a battleship.

The entire edifice was completed on January 15, 1943, a mere 16 months after groundbreaking. The Pentagon, only five stories high, is huge—it has three times as much space as the Empire State Building. The Pentagon's sheer amplitude has long contributed to its effectiveness as a great security blanket. Now that has changed, just a little. It took the magnitude of September 11, a day as large and overpowering as the Pentagon itself, to crack that security, to wound the country's enormous protector.

Three shifts of workers toiled 24 hours a day, every day. This photo was taken in 1942.

on the towers. In 1974 the French aerialist Philippe
Petit walked a tightrope that was stretched between
the north and south towers. The next year, a para-
chutist jumped from the roof, and two years later
a rock climber scaled the sheer walls of the south
tower. When Hollywood remade *King Kong* in
1976, the Empire State Building was out, the World
Trade Center was in. New Yorkers love stuff like
that—they love notoriety—and they love, as well,
outrageous facts to know and tell. Did you know
the buildings weigh more than 1.5 million tons?
they would ask (or the tour guides would). That
they contain 198 miles of heating ducts, 23,000
fluorescent lightbulbs, 10 million square feet of
space, 43,600 windows, 194 passenger elevators?
Did you know the express travels 27 feet per second and reaches the 110th floor in 4.8 minutes?

New Yorkers and other denizens of the global
village did, finally, come to love the towers.

Unfortunately, the greatest of buildings—pal-
pable symbols of a successful society—often stand
in harm's way. On February 23, 1993, six people
were killed and a thousand injured when bombs
were detonated in a parking garage beneath the
Center, leading to life sentences for six Islamic
extremists. But the building held.

Much earlier, on July 28, 1945, a B-25 bomber
got lost in the fog and slammed into the 79th floor
of the Empire State Building. Fourteen lives were
lost and there was massive damage, but that
building, too, held. When the World Trade Center
was in design, the Empire State incident was
recalled, and the Twin Towers were built to with-
stand a blow from a big jetliner—the biggest jetliner being flown at the time, which was, of course,
many years, and many lifetimes, ago.

John Annerino

When, on September 11, 2001, the United States was attacked at home, the original date of infamy was immediately invoked. Franklin Delano Roosevelt's historic words, spoken in the wake of the Pearl Harbor bombing, were attached by commentators and military leaders alike to this new and dreadful assault. Ultimately, President George W. Bush took the final step and said that, yes, as with the terrible blow struck in Hawaii 60 years ago, this latest infamous deed was nothing less than . . .

"An

Act of War"

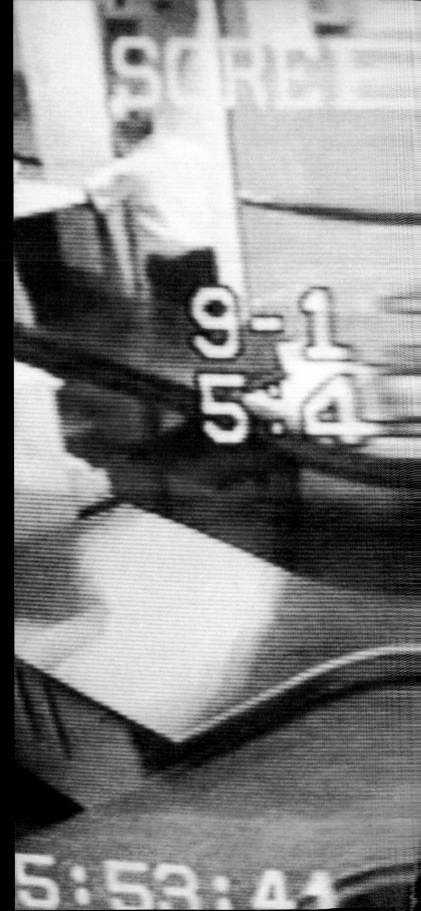

5:45 **a.m.** Mohamed Atta and Abdulaziz Alomari pass through a security check in Portland, Me., preparing to board a flight that will take them to Boston.

6:00 President George W. Bush awakes at the Colony, a tennis resort in Longboat Key, Fla.

6:00 Primary Day election polls for mayor and other positions open in New York. Mayor Rudolph W. Giuliani cannot run again, owing to term limits.

8:00 American Airlines Flight 11 leaves Logan Airport in Boston bound for Los Angeles with 81 passengers and 11 crewmembers.

8:14 United Flight 175 to Los Angeles departs Boston with 56 passengers and nine crewmembers.

8:21 American Flight 77 to Los Angeles departs Washington Dulles International Airport with 58 passengers and six crew on board.

8:35 The Federal Aviation Administration alerts NORAD that American Flight 11 has been hijacked after taking off from Boston.

8:42 United Airlines Flight 93 to San Francisco takes off from Newark Airport in New Jersey with 38 passengers and seven crew on board.

8:43 The FAA notifies NORAD that United Flight 175 from Boston to L.A. has also been hijacked.

8:44 NORAD scrambles two F-15 fighters from Otis Air National Guard Base in Falmouth, Mass.

9:02 Cameras trained on the burning north tower capture live the horrifying view of another jet, United Flight 175 with its 65 passengers and crew, blasting into floors 78 to 87 of the Trade Center's south tower in a tumultuous explosion. It is instantly clear that nothing on this day has been accidental.

Evan Fairbanks was
working at nearby
Trinity Church
when he heard an
explosion and went to
a window. "It looked
like the Yankees'
parade. Stuff was just
raining down." He
grabbed a video
camera and ran
outside and captured
this sequence of
Flight 175 crashing
into the south tower.
Fairbanks didn't know
the man in the
foreground, who is
leaning on a truck. In
front of the man is a
boombox that is
playing a news
account of the attack.

9:05

The President is sitting in with a second-grade class when Andrew Card whispers to him that yet another airplane has struck the Twin Towers.

9:08 The FAA closes all New York–area airports and "sterilizes" the airspace over the city.

9:09 Mayor Giuliani is racing downtown in his limousine, having received word moments after the first attack. He checks in at a fire command post in the World Trade Center that would later be crushed. Giuliani and aides then make their perilous way a block north to set up a communications center at 75 Barclay Street, but debris cascading from the ceiling forces them to seek another location.

9:12 Bush leaves the school and is in touch with New York officials as well as Vice President Dick Cheney at the White House.

9:20 The FBI announces that reports of planes being hijacked are under investigation.

9:21 The Port Authority of New York and New Jersey orders that all bridges and tunnels in the metropolitan area be closed.

9:24 The FAA notifies NORAD that a third jet, American Flight 77, bound from Washington to Los Angeles, has been hijacked. NORAD launches two F-16 fighters from Langley Air Force Base in Virginia to intercept the airliner.

9:25 The New York Stock Exchange delays all trading.

9:26 For the first time in history, the FAA orders all nonmilitary planes grounded and cancels all flights in the U.S.

9:27 New York City airports are shut down.

9:29 First reports of casualties indicate that at least six people are dead and 1,000 injured.

9:29 Rescue workers and fire marshals are massed at the World Trade Center as the upper floors are ablaze. On a typical day, 50,000 people work in the Trade Center, and as many as 100,000 visit.

9:30 With students and teachers looking on, President Bush, having been briefed by National Security Adviser Condoleezza Rice, delivers his first official remarks on the catastrophe: "We have had a national tragedy. Two airplanes have crashed into the World Trade Center in an apparent terrorist attack on our country." He orders "a full-scale investigation to hunt down and to find those folks who committed these acts" and says he will immediately return to Washington.

9:30 The New York Stock Exchange is evacuated, and trading is suspended.

9:32 All financial markets in the United States are closed.

BEAR ON A BIKE

Black, oily smoke—another grim reminder of Pearl Harbor—billows from the jet-fuel-torched Twin Towers as the city, the nation, the world, watch in disbelief. The smoke would remain a nasty element that would cling to New York City for many long days to come.

Andy Levin/Corbis Sygma

The north tower: Some people, trapped in a nightmare of fire and smoke, decide to control their own fate. The scene was among the most disturbing of a hellish day.

Richard Drew/AP

CHRONICLE OF AN ESCAPE

John Labriola, in his capacity as a technical services consultant, was at work on the 71st floor of 1 World Trade when the first plane hit. "The building rocked in one direction, then shuddered back and forth," he remembers. "It felt like it moved five or six feet in each direction." Out the window Labriola saw papers floating against an azure sky "like in a ticker-tape parade," but also "fireballs and debris raining down." He made for a stairwell and, as a longtime photography enthusiast, took out his ever-present digital camera.

“People were covering their mouths against the smoke. It was very hot. We were slipping on the sweat of those who had gone before. When the second plane hit, we felt it, but had no idea. Then someone got news on his pager that a plane had hit each tower. Around the 35th floor we started meeting the stream of firefighters walking up. None of them said a word. I can't stop thinking about the look in their eyes, how heroic they were. I learned later that Mike Kehoe (above) barely made it out.”

> **We had to press into a single file so the firefighters could march past. They were carrying unbelievable loads of equipment, and were already exhausted by the time we started seeing them. The people going down were very polite to one another. They helped others who needed it, and they waited for each other. One man literally carried a woman down the steps because she was unable to make it on her own. Two others helped a guy on crutches.**

> As we went down, there was water flowing in the stairwell, creating rapids down the stairs. When we finally got to the lobby we could see teams of firefighters in a staging area, waiting their turn to go up. I pray some of them made it out. There was a courtyard outside but we weren't allowed to go out there. Windows had been shattered, and the courtyard was loaded with debris. They must have determined that it was too dangerous for us to cross. So we were directed to the escalators.

There were two escalators going down into the mall under Tower 1. At the bottom we had to run through a waterfall. Water was falling everywhere—eight to 10 inches in some places. Rescuers were strategically placed throughout the area, shouting at us, keeping us focused on where to go. Many of the stores down in the mall had windows blown out. All along the way there were emergency workers urging us on. It was very loud down there from the water, the crowd, the shouting.

> **I went up an escalator and emerged onto Church Street. Fifty minutes later, I was finally outside. As I stepped into the light I heard yelling: 'Don't look up! Keep moving!' I looked up. It was unreal. I saw someone fall. I stopped looking up. I wasn't sure where to go. I headed south on Broadway. The doors to Trinity Church were open so I went inside. A priest was leading prayers. I knelt to pray. The first building fell. Stained glass windows that were filled with color turned inky black.**

9:41

American Flight 77, en route from Dulles Airport in Washington, D.C., to Los Angeles with 64 people aboard, crashes into the Pentagon in Arlington, Va., a suburb of Washington. The nerve center of the U.S. military erupts in flames and a portion of the structure collapses. Defense Secretary Donald Rumsfeld is in the building but escapes harm. Evacuation commences. The plane was traveling so low that it clipped lampposts on roads around the Pentagon, and eyewitnesses report that it powered up just before impact. The fighter planes from Langley were still 12 minutes, or 105 miles, away when the Pentagon was hit.

9:43 Abu Dhabi TV reports a call from the Democratic Front for the Liberation of Palestine claiming responsibility for directing two planes into the Trade Center. However, officials of that group later deny making the claim.

9:45 The White House is evacuated.

9:48 The U.S. Capitol is evacuated after bomb threats. Other federal buildings in D.C. close.

Larry Downing/Reuters/Getty (2)

9:50

The 110-story south tower of the World Trade Center suddenly, and simply, collapses, a victim of the steel-melting heat of the inferno. Witnesses report hearing a sucking sound and then an incredible surge of air as the floors pancake downward. A vast cloud of smoke, dirt and debris forms and slowly spreads from the building. Countless pieces of office paper drift into Brooklyn and out over the Hudson River.

9:55 Bush hastily departs on an evasive route for Barksdale Air Force Base, outside Shreveport, La.

9:58 An emergency dispatcher in Pennsylvania receives a call from a passenger on United Flight 93 out of Newark who says, "We are being hijacked, we are being hijacked!"

10:00 Aboard *Air Force One* en route to Louisiana, Bush calls Vice President Cheney and puts America's military on high-alert status. The President sifts through updates from his staff, including an erroneous report that a car bomb had detonated at the State Department.

With the Municipal Building in the rear, dumbstruck New Yorkers on a Tuesday morning in Park Row behold the demise of the south tower.

Patrick Witty

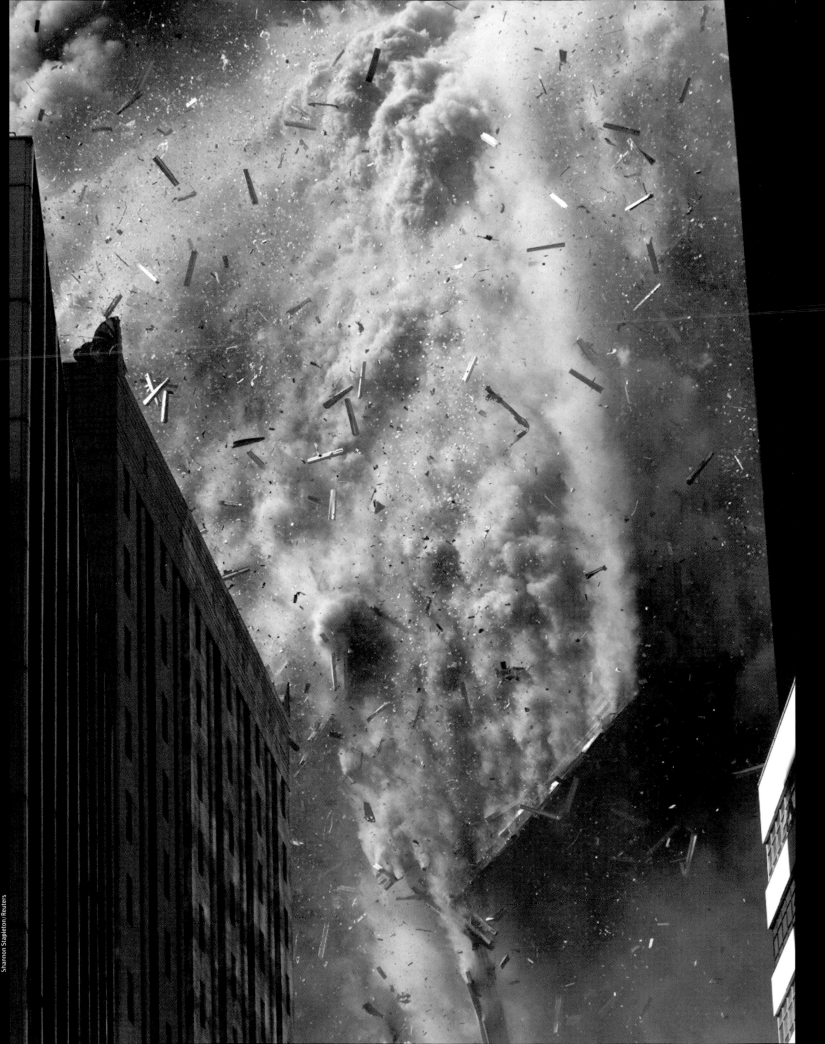

With the south tower disintegrating and the north tower wrapped in flames and spewing smoke, frightened, bewildered people surge northward on Church Street.

Susan Meiselas/Magnum

"If anyone can hear me, make some noise and we'll come help you." Having called out his plea, this man at the corner of Church and Cortlandt streets, fire extinguisher in hand, awaits a response. As with so many, he wants only to somehow help.

Doug Kanter/AFP

Ruth Fremson/The New York Times

Shannon Stapleton/Reuters

A police officer in the Stage Door Deli III on Vesey Street reaches within for strength and sanity following the crumbling of the south tower. Above: Descending a stairway at ground level of the Trade Center plaza, evacuees from the north tower grapple with a daunting scenario.

10:00

United Flight 93, traveling from Newark to San Francisco with 45 people aboard, crashes in Shanksville, Pa. (right), 80 miles southeast of Pittsburgh, having turned back from its westward heading.

Kamenko Pajic/AP

10:08 Across from the White House, in Lafayette Park, Secret Service agents are deployed with automatic rifles.

10:10 A portion of the Pentagon caves in.

10:13 In New York, the United Nations building is evacuated.

10:22 In Washington, the State and Justice departments are evacuated, along with the World Bank.

10:24 The FAA reports that all transatlantic aircraft flying into the U.S. are being diverted to Canada.

Mark Stahl

10:28

The north tower of the World Trade Center collapses into itself in a fury of smoke and mayhem, sending vast amounts of debris into the surrounding streets. Hundreds of firefighters are trapped and killed. The huge communications antenna at the summit plummets like a rocket gone wrong,

Gulnara Samoilova/AP

10:29

In apocalyptic scenes, throngs of desperate people flee the chaotic area, spreading into Broadway and Greenwich, West and Liberty streets. A dense, hurtful miasma of dust suffuses lower Manhattan. "There are no words to describe this," says CBS television newsman Dan Rather, who stops talking for many long seconds.

10:30 New York Governor George E. Pataki declares a state of emergency.

10:41 The President is aboard *Air Force One,* which is headed toward Jacksonville to join up with jets providing air cover. On the phone from a protected area of the White House, Vice President Cheney presses Bush not to return quickly to Washington.

10:46 U.S. Secretary of State Colin Powell cuts short his trip to Latin America to return to the United States.

10:50 Nerves are taut around the Pentagon as rumors spread that a second attack plane is coming.

10:53 New York's primary elections are postponed.

10:54 Israel evacuates all diplomatic missions.

Just minutes after the collapse of the south tower, this firefighter is being rushed to a treatment center. When the photographer asked if he could take his picture, the firefighter barely had the strength to utter, "Sure, it's okay."

Klaus Reisinger/Editing-Server

Fire department chaplain Mychal Judge is carried from the disaster.
He was slain when struck in the head by debris. Father Judge had been
kneeling, giving the last rites to a firefighter who had been killed by a
falling body. Because the 68-year-old chaplain's body was the first to
be released from Ground Zero, his death certificate bore the number 1.

Shannon Stapleton/Reuters

Mary Altaffer

11:00 New York City Mayor Giuliani (above) tells people to stay home and orders lower Manhattan evacuated.

11:16 The Centers for Disease Control and Prevention states that emergency-response teams are being assembled.

11:18 American Airlines confirms that two of its planes have been hijacked and presumed crashed.

11:45 With the U.S. military on nuclear alert, the President arrives at Barksdale Air Force Base in Louisiana. Reporters are asked to keep their cell phones off, to conceal his location. From a conference room, Bush calls, among others, Cheney, Rumsfeld and New York Senator Charles Schumer.

12:04 p.m. Los Angeles International Airport, the destination of three of the crashed airplanes, is evacuated.

12:15 The U.S. announces that its borders with Mexico and Canada have been closed.

12:15 San Francisco International Airport, the destination of Flight 93, is evacuated and shut down.

12:36 In a taped statement from Barksdale Air Force Base, President Bush says that U.S. armed forces are on worldwide "high-alert status" and that all appropriate security precautions have been taken. "Make no mistake, the United States will hunt down and punish those responsible for these cowardly acts."

12:55 Taliban officials, speaking from Afghanistan, deny any responsibility for the attacks. "What happened in the United States was not a job of ordinary people. It could have been the work of governments," says Taliban spokesperson Abdul Hai Mutmaen.

Police, fire and other emergency rescue teams confront a bedlam of steel and stone at Ground Zero.

1:15 Bush departs for *Air Force One* in a camouflaged Humvee. While en route to Offutt Air Force Base near Omaha, he talks to Cheney again and schedules a four p.m. meeting of his national security staff. He also talks to Giuliani and Pataki. "I know your heart is broken and your city is strained, and anything we can do, let me know," Bush says.

1:27 A state of emergency is declared in Washington, D.C.

1:44 The Pentagon says five warships and two aircraft carriers will leave the U.S. Naval Station in Norfolk, Va., to protect the East Coast from further attack and to reduce the number of ships in port. The two carriers, the USS *George Washington* and the USS *John F. Kennedy,* are headed for New York. The other ships are frigates and guided missile destroyers capable of shooting down aircraft.

2:30 The FAA announces there will be no commercial air traffic permitted until noon EDT Wednesday at the earliest.

2:49 At a news conference, Giuliani says that subway and bus service are partially restored in New York City. Asked about the number of people killed, Giuliani says, "I don't think we want to speculate about that—more than any of us can bear."

Mario Tama/Getty

Peering into hell: This rescue team of firefighters will soon unearth two of their fallen comrades.

2:50 President Bush arrives at Offutt Air Force Base in Nebraska, where he descends into a cinder-block bunker. There, he teleconferences with the eight-member National Security Council. Vice President Cheney—who had suggested Bush go to Offutt—and National Security Adviser Condoleezza Rice are connected from a secure facility at the White House. Defense Secretary Rumsfeld has remained at the Pentagon.

4:00 U.S. officials say there are "good indications" based on "new and specific" information that Saudi militant Osama bin Laden, suspected of coordinating the bombings of two U.S. embassies in Africa in 1998 and the October 2000 bombing of the USS *Cole*, is involved in the latest attacks.

4:10 Building 7 of the World Trade Center complex is reportedly on fire.

4:25 The American Stock Exchange, Nasdaq and the New York Stock Exchange say they will remain closed Wednesday.

Dennis Van Tine/London Features/UDV

David Bohrer/The White House

Eric Draper/The White House (2)

4:36

The President leaves Offutt Air Force Base aboard *Air Force One* to return to Washington. While in the air (above), he renews his telephone link with, at right, National Security Adviser Rice (center) and Vice President Cheney (right). The Chief Executive also makes time to call First Lady Laura Bush and says, "I'm coming home. See you at the White House." He then works with aides on his speech to be delivered that evening.

5:20 The 47-story Building 7 of the World Trade Center collapses. The structure, already evacuated, was damaged when the Twin Towers across the street fell earlier in the day. Other nearby buildings remain ablaze.

5:30 U.S. officials say the plane that crashed in Pennsylvania could have been headed for one of three possible targets: Camp David, the White House or the U.S. Capitol.

6:00 Explosions heard in Kabul, Afghanistan, are credited to the Northern Alliance, a group fighting the Taliban in the country's ongoing civil war. The U.S. denies any involvement.

6:10 Giuliani urges New Yorkers to stay home Wednesday if at all possible.

6:40 Rumsfeld holds a news conference in the Pentagon and says the building is operational. "It will be in business tomorrow."

6:54 Bush arrives at the White House aboard the helicopter *Marine One* and is scheduled to address the nation at 8:30 p.m. The President had landed at Andrews Air Force Base in Maryland with a fighter jet escort. Laura Bush greets him, having arrived earlier by motorcade from a "secure location."

7:45 The New York Police Department says that at least 78 officers are missing. The city also states that as many as half of the first 400 firefighters on the scene were killed.

8:30 President Bush speaks to the nation on television, saying "thousands of lives were suddenly ended by evil," and asks for prayers for the families and friends of Tuesday's victims. "These acts shattered steel, but they cannot dent the steel of American resolve." The President says the United States will make no distinction between the terrorists who committed the acts and those who harbor them.

8:35 Bush attends a security meeting (left).

9:57 Giuliani closes New York City schools for Wednesday and says no more volunteers are needed for the evening's rescue efforts. He says there is hope that people are still alive. He also says that power is out on the West Side of Manhattan and adds that health department tests show no airborne chemical agents.

10:21 Bush calls an end to the security meeting. Secret Service radios carry the news that the President has gone home to bed: "Trailblazer. Second floor of the residence."

Eyewitness
James Nachtwey at Ground Zero

Photo of Nachtwey by Graham Morrison

Although his apartment is in lower Manhattan, James Nachtwey is always elsewhere. You might say that he travels the globe as a professional photographer—perhaps the world's preeminent chronicler of war—but Nachtwey feels he goes as a witness. It is a role he is driven to play; he doesn't think he has a choice in the matter. "My life is not balanced," he says candidly. "It's very unbalanced, in fact. Being a war photographer precludes what would be a normal family life. But then, I've never aspired to be normal. It's just not my personal makeup. I've weighed what I do against a balanced life, and I've made my decision."

So he's never home, but he is always in the right place at the right time to record eerily beautiful images of violence and injustice. His colleagues wonder at his uncanny tendency to be at the precise crossroads in Hebron, Rwanda or Bosnia to make the picture that will turn the world's head.

Jim Nachtwey flew home to New York City from Europe on the evening of September 10. The next morning he was startled by "a crash, as if a huge sheet of metal had dropped on my roof." He ran up to the roof, camera in hand, and started shooting pictures of the smoking north tower. His instinct, as always, was to get closer, to reach Ground Zero. So he was running down the stairs as the south tower was hit.

He reached the financial district in minutes, moving in and around the scene before authorities began to try to keep people out. "It felt familiar. I had seen things like this before," he says. "But it was also the largest single act of destruction I had ever witnessed. And since I'm an American who lived close by—in the gravitational field of this tragedy—it had a different effect. I had an anger about it."

Nachtwey is regularly moved by what he sees, but while he lets emotion dictate which scene might be effective—which picture is most worth making—he never lets it disrupt the task at hand. He worked through the day until it was dark, at times dodging debris, constantly piecing together the story. Then he walked out of Ground Zero and back into his neighborhood, which had been transformed. "It was now a war zone," he says. "At night I had to burn candles. I would cross six checkpoints to get home. It was just like being in Grozny or Mostar—exactly those conditions. But this was my home."

“ I was making a frame with the church in the foreground—it was about the church, and the injured building behind it—when the first tower just exploded and collapsed. It became a different picture. I realized all of a sudden that a tidal wave of steel girders and debris and smoke was bearing down on me. I had enough time to run for cover, and escaped. ”

" A few other photographers and I were standing right under the second tower when it fell. I didn't have any idea it was going to, even though the first one had. It listed west, and I was on the east side of it. It was fortunate for me, unfortunate for others. There was an avalanche of girders, clouds of smoke coming straight down on me. I had a few seconds to do something or I was going to be killed. A door to the Millenium Hotel on Church Street was open and I dashed in there. I realized all this stuff was going to be taken out—the windows, the lobby. I was cornered. I got into an elevator, a small steel cubicle for protection. One second after I got in, steel and glass poured down. I was okay. There was a construction worker there, and we thought the building had fallen on our hotel and we were trapped in a pocket. But we weren't sure, we couldn't see anything. We got on our hands and knees and crawled toward the entrance. He said, 'If God is with us we might make it out of here.' He was calling for others: 'Need help?' No one else was there. Back outside, the ash was so thick. Absolutely pitch-black. I couldn't see anything. My mouth was full of ash, my eyes felt full of mud. I walked back in toward Ground Zero. These guys were walking out. "

"I realized I had to get to the site of the tower lying in the street. So I made my way toward it through the smoke. It was very deserted there. People had fled. Those who were still there, they didn't know what to do—I remember one man was just wandering in a daze. There was debris everywhere, crushed trucks, crushed cars. A ghost town with all these wrecked buildings, streets and vehicles."

" This was in the World Financial Center. All the glass had been blown out, so you could just walk in. It was very haunting in there, that one man like a ghost. **"**

" The story came to us in bits and pieces during the day. I thought maybe there had been bombs, but we quickly learned they were planes. We heard about the Pentagon. I started to think the pictures would serve to document a crucial historical watershed. I think America is now part of the world in a way in which it never has been before. **"**

The Attacker

Battered Flag

Avengers

I Plead For Peace

Artist, poet, filmmaker, New Yorker and longtime LIFE photographer Gordon Parks was moved to remember the day in word and imagery.

Bottomless Tuesday by Gordon Parks

America—a wounded eagle,
shrieks revenge for a murderous attack.
Terror and anger race our shores together.
Our stalwart lady of liberty stands watchful,
scanning the horizon, awaiting storms
that are uncertain as the resting place
    of a falling leaf.
Death clouds hover in blood-spattered skies.
Lion-hearted rescuers search the rubble—
counting, grasping whatever was left—
an ear, a foot, a finger with a wedding band.
On and on they go, looking for signs of death.
Peace, trapped in the cadence of our star-spangled past,
distances itself from these battering days and nights.
Abused by history—a blurred hope departed.
"Prepare for sustained assault! We are at war!"
The commander's battle-cry from Camp David
burned with resolve and determination.

Yet, a ghostly past watches, knowing well
that within man's hostility toward man
there lies a forgetfulness of young flesh
    being blown apart
under banners of patriotism.
Consider the youthful warriors
before your diplomacy sees them dead.
Somebody on both sides—listen!

Let us develop a preference for love
over that of missiles and poisoned air.
With fanatical design, the attackers
found chinks in this nation's armor.
Everywhere, in their dark world of holes,
    guns
are stealthily looking for them.
"We will find the terrorists before they strike!"
To those of us who remember,
this warning may seem somewhat reassuring.
Of those dead, who have no answers,
Better not to expect any questions.

If we were able to speak with the dead,
to those who so nobly searched the rubble,
and vanished under smoke and flame,
We should tell them their feet walked
where very few feet have walked before.
If, with their grieving ones left behind,
we could discuss the depth of their sorrow,
we should ask them to have a talk with faith—
    and hold on to it
with the arrival of every lonely night and day.
Ours is a planet with a multitude
of beliefs, languages and worshippers.
No one should desert it until they have found
what GOD put us here to find—LOVE!
Even death should not keep it from growing!

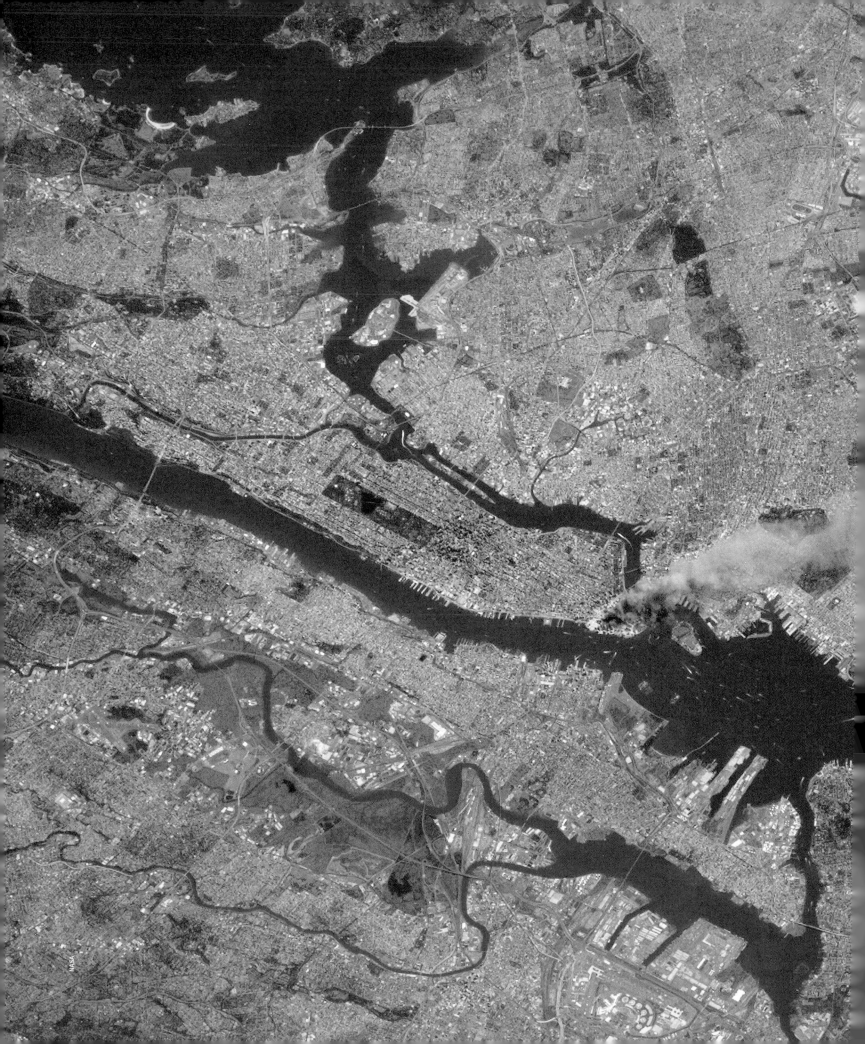

Central Park

New Jersey

Manhattan   Queens

Brooklyn

COLLAPSED

1 1 World Trade Center

2 2 World Trade Center

3 7 World Trade Center

4 North Bridge

5 St. Nicholas Church

PARTIALLY COLLAPSED

6 WTC Marriott Hotel

7 4 World Trade Center

8 5 World Trade Center

9 6 World Trade Center

SUBSTANTIAL DAMAGE

10 30 West Broadway

11 Verizon Building

12 3 World Financial Center

13 Winter Garden

14 90 West Street

15 Bankers Trust Building

FACADE DAMAGE

16 One Liberty Plaza

17 22 Cortlandt Street

18 Millenium Hilton Hotel

19 Federal Office Building

20 2 World Financial Center

21 1 World Financial Center

TIME graphic by Joe Zeff and Ed Gabel

Several buildings were obliterated, others toppled. The Winter Garden, a sublime atrium linking two World Financial Center buildings, was wrecked. Its owners vowed to restore it.

Eric J. Tilford/AP/U.S. Navy

Aftermath

The dust did not clear, of course, nor did the smoke—not soon. And on the morning of the 12th, Americans awoke to discover that the nightmare would not go away. "You must go see it," New Yorkers, politicians and world leaders were urged. When they did, first taking in the spectacle from afar and then looking in, they were amazed. Horrified.

The disaster area covered 16 acres and contained an estimated 1.4 million tons of debris. In the first month of the cleanup, 291,879 tons were hauled from the site in dump trucks. The first few weeks of the operation cost more than $200 million, and the price tag for the project, which might take a year, could reach $5 billion.

Lennie Falcon

Nearly every building in the area took a hit. The World Financial Center, by the Hudson River, had windows blown out. Bankers Trust on Liberty Street was gouged by a chunk of the south tower. The Millenium Hilton (opposite) on Church Street was pockmarked by shrapnel.

Anton Oparin/Corbis SABA

Frank Schwere/Matrix

Dust and ash coated all, lending scenes a terrible beauty. O'Hara's on Cedar Street was desolate, while Brooks Brothers on Church Street served as a temporary morgue. A week after the attack, thousands of residents remained displaced, including those of a Cedar Street flat where the tea had gone cold.

Edward Keating/The New York Times

A Blow

The prayer wall at Bellevue
Hospital in New York City

to America's Heart

James Rexroad

Did they know the complexity of the harm they were causing? The psychological as well as physical and emotional pain? Were they, indeed, as smart as that?

Other possible targets and intended targets notwithstanding, in bringing down the Twin Towers of the World Trade Center and demolishing a section of the Pentagon, the terrorists inflicted symbolic as well as literal wounds upon the multichambered heart of America. The gravest damage was done in a place where, long ago, ideas of liberty were sanctified and where, ever since the country's founding, a mighty economic engine has been housed. The strike in Washington, D.C., was even less subtle, tearing at the very notion of U.S. power and might. Southernmost Manhattan and the immense military complex in Virginia are places of the mind as well as physical buildings and grounds. History, as it often does, lends critical context.

The tip of the island is where New York was born; the city, in fact, predates the name. In 1609, Englishman Henry Hudson, employed by the Dutch to find a Northwest Passage to the Orient, sailed past Manhattan and up the river that now bears his name. During the next short while, several Dutch trading posts were established in the Hudson River Valley, and in 1621 merchants banded together as the Dutch West India Company. Four years later, Dutch colonists started work on a fort quite near

> **"The gravest damage was done in a place where, long ago, ideas of liberty were sanctified."**

where the Trade Center would one day rise, and constructed the first buildings of a town that would fan out north of the barricades. They named the settlement New Amsterdam. In 1626 the Dutch bought the whole of the island from the Indians for goods worth 60 guilders, or about $24—an early example of the infinity of transactions that would take place near what we now know as Wall Street. It really was a wall during the Dutch heyday, intended to protect the colony's northern border. New Amsterdam was a small place back then, only about as big as the area covered by the maps of Ground Zero.

The Netherlands and England fought each other on the seas almost constantly from the early 1650s into the 1670s, and when the cannon smoke finally cleared, New Amsterdam was among the spoils surrendered to the English in a peace treaty. The new New York burgeoned under British rule and, with Boston and Philadelphia, was one of the colonies' three major cities by the time of the Revolution. The British controlled it for most of the war, but when the colonies prevailed, New York was the site of several signal instances in the birth of a great nation. On December 4, 1783, at Fraunces Tavern on Pearl Street, the downtown hangout of the Sons of Liberty, General George Washington, having earlier made his triumphal entry into the city, bade an emotional farewell to his officers: "I most devoutly wish that your later days may be as prosperous and happy as your former ones have been glorious and honorable." New York was the capital of the United States from 1785 to 1790, and Washington was inaugurated as the first President there in 1789. On September 25th of that year, within yards of where the Twin Towers would one day rise and fall, the first 10 amendments to the Constitution—including those protecting liberties of speech, assembly, religion and the right to bear arms—were proposed.

From 1785 to 1788 the Departments of Foreign Affairs, Treasury and War were headquartered at Fraunces, and the nation's grand Treasury building was subsequently constructed hard by the "call market" that would evolve into the New York Stock Exchange. All of this history and all of these ghosts inhabited the neighborhood of the World Trade Center, a unifying symbol of the whole—and of America's outward reach to the world.

The Pentagon, too, was a building of coalescence, even if it was built on less storied ground. The War Office couldn't be housed in a saloon forever, and eventually found its way to Washington. But the Navy split off and there were several other changes in organization and responsibility over the years. Eventually, nerve centers committed to the national defense were scattered throughout the capital. In 1941, just in time for World War II, work began on a massive complex to be built along the swampy western shore of the Potomac. The Pentagon was open for business not long after Pearl Harbor.

Symbolic architecture is always transcendent in that it is never just about the building, and it is always a target for those who disagree. When British troops marched through Washington in 1814, they made sure to burn the White House and the Capitol, the two representative buildings of American democracy, and during the Kristallnacht sweeps in 1938, the Nazis desecrated synagogues. America's enemies had already announced with the 1993 bombing that the Twin Towers were targets, and what America-hater wouldn't want a shot at the Pentagon?

The terrorists attacked not only American institutions and cultural history, they also attacked American principles and, of course, people. In the long aftermath of 9/11/01, *The New York Times* ran an unbroken series of pages filled with biographies of the missing and lists of the newly confirmed dead. Pick any one of the pages and a message becomes clear. Missing: Campbell, McEneaney, Hardy, Angrisani, Abate, Aiken, Echtermann, Virgilio, Goldstein, Burke, Vidal, Flecha, Fitzsimons, Goody, Siskopoulos, Legro. The same day's dead: Chung, Fox, Gonzalez, Guadalupe, Halderman, Hughes, Leveen, McCabe, McDowell, Petrocelli, Sayegh, Yuen. That was—that is—America. Aboard American Flight 11 out of Boston: Bouchard, Dimeglio, Filipov, Jalbert, Jones. Aboard United Flight 93 out of Newark: Garcia, Green, Miller, Wainio, Welsh. At the Pentagon: Caballero, Getzfred, Murphy, Schlegel, Young. The United States' way of democracy had, over more than two centuries, fostered the world's first great international nation. It has often been commented upon that the hijackers were able to operate effectively because they were moving in a free society, malevolently abusing America's trust. That's true enough, but a more telling point might be the near unanimity of the world's condemnation of the terrorists' deed. In the new millennium, we are the world, and the world is us. It is, largely, on our side. For the terrorists to be right, everybody else everywhere must be wrong—and that's not the way it is.

So, then, on September 11, 2001:

Democracy was attacked.

Liberty was assaulted.

The global economy was staggered.

American might was confronted.

The terrorists with their particular targets: Did they know the complexity of the harm they were inflicting? Were they, indeed, as smart as that?

In one way, yes. They were smart enough to know that these places meant more to America

> "The terrorists attacked not only American institutions and cultural history, they also attacked American principles and, of course, they attacked people."

On his first visit to New York, President Bush is greeted by Mayor Giuliani (left) and Governor Pataki.

than other buildings filled with workers. Certainly the hijackers intended to terrify and to dishearten by attacking our society's all-but-sacred institutions. America is weak, their leaders had told them. America will cower in the face of our ferocity and the boldness of our strike.

Here, they miscalculated. In this belief, they were not so smart. As quickly as walls fell, Americans rose. Throughout the land, millions of flags unfurled and thousands of volunteers rushed to aid the victims, their families and the heroes toiling inexhaustibly in the devil's dens known, in both Washington and New York, as Ground Zero. Planes and battleships were mobilized, troops called up, and, in a global police action, hundreds of suspects were detained. Before a shot was fired, the new war was begun.

Immediately after the original date of infamy, 12/7/41, Japanese admiral Yamamoto Isoroku, the primary architect of the raid on Pearl Harbor, observed ominously, "I fear all we have done is to awaken a sleeping giant and fill him with a terrible resolve." On the 12th of September, 2001, might Osama bin Laden, perhaps hiding deep within one of his Afghan redoubts, have been wondering the same?

The answer is of little consequence. What matters is, America is roused, united and, as of October 7, fully engaged. That, finally, is the legacy of September 11. The country that survived a blow to its heart is now pledged to reinvigorate American liberty, to show what it means to live in the land of the free and the home of the brave. It is a decent thing to do. It is a way to honor the dead.

Union Square in New York City, two miles from Ground Zero, became a gathering place for people to share their grief. There was a shrine of remembrance and regular candlelight vigils for the dead and missing.

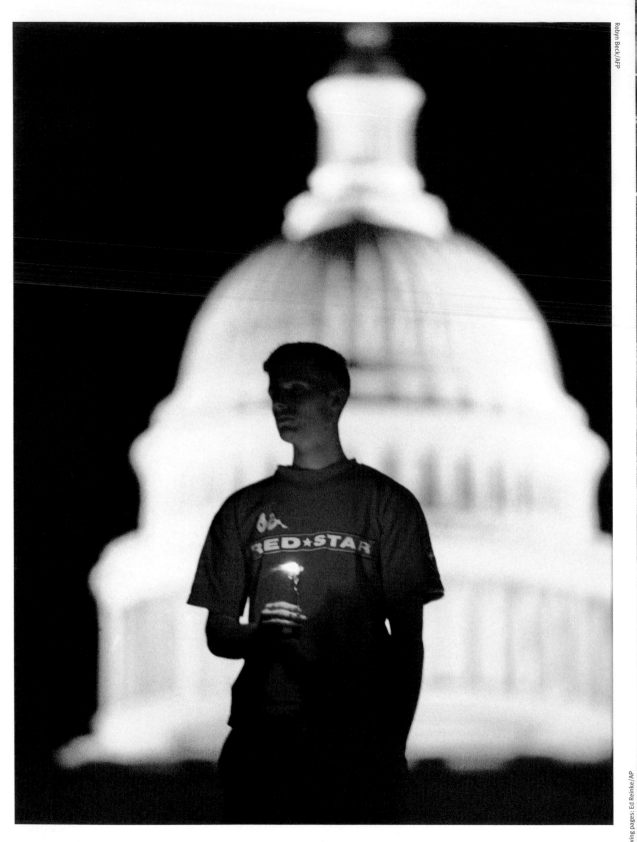

At the Capitol, the light of liberty contrasted with the light of mourning. The Stars and Stripes sprouted along every highway and byway (right, in Pennsylvania). Following pages: Before a football game in Lexington, Ky., the national anthem set off a frenzy of flag-waving. From sea to shining sea, flags fluttered, rippling vehemently from car antennas or sending a more poignant message from half-staff.

Heroism
Large and Small

We can never know the extent of heroism displayed that day. It reached from moments of graciousness far removed from the scenes of death and destruction to lost-forever gestures between one dying soul and another. Based on what we do know, heroism, gallantry and courage were general in New York, Washington and the skies above Pennsylvania. Some of these stories are oft-told, others have hardly been commented upon. Together they stand as testament to something good in the human spirit, and something noble in the American character.

Bottom: Courtesy of CNN. Top: Luke Frazza/AFP

Lisa Beamer (above, left) didn't learn of her husband's heroism until she received a call from GTE Airfone operator Lisa Jefferson.

Taking Back the Plane

"I know I'm not going to get out of this."

"I want to tell you I love you."

"I know we're going to die. Some of us are going to do something about it."

"We're going to rush the hijackers."

The phone calls made by Todd Beamer to a GTE Airfone operator, Mark Bingham to his mother, and Tom Burnett Jr. and Jeremy Glick to their wives constitute a remarkable chronicle of death foretold and a gripping record of heroism rising. United Airlines Flight 93 out of Newark, N.J., originally destined for San Francisco, was in the air longer than any of the other three hijacked jets—an hour and 18 minutes in all—and that time allowed several

Courtesy Lyzbeth Glick

strong young men to form a unit of resistance that would, finally, foil the hijackers' evil intent.

There may have been more than just the four. Lorne Lyles, a police officer in Fort Myers, Fla., believes that his wife, flight attendant CeeCee Lyles, herself a former cop, would have been part of any plot to jump the hijackers. But we have evidence regarding the four men, evidence supplied by phone conversations. If the hijacking of Flight 93 was a low-tech affair done with knives, boxcutters and the threat of a bomb, then the counterattack on the hijackers, as well as the subsequent uncovering of what might have happened, was post-modern, with information being shuttled to and from the plane via cell phones and Airfones.

Tom Burnett, CEO of a medical research company and a father of three, called his wife, Deena, in San Ramon, Calif., not long after the plane had been hijacked. "How are you?" she asked. "Bad," he said, and told her the news. "This is my flight number. Call the authorities." Deena did so, then received another call from Tom. This time, she told him what she knew about the horror in New York City—planes being flown into both of the Twin Towers. Tom, for his part, reported: "They've knifed a guy. They say there's a bomb." He again told her

Philip Greenberg

Jeremy Glick was fiercely devoted to his infant daughter, Emerson. His wife, Lyzbeth, seen here at his memorial service, felt Jeremy's presence on the plane was destiny, "to stop some of the evil."

Judy Griesedieck

Deena and Tom, married 10 years, had three daughters, twins Madison and Halley, five, and Anna, three. The girls have asked if they can call their dad, in heaven.

to pass along the information to law enforcement.

Lyzbeth Glick had been watching the Trade Center drama on her parents' TV at their home in upstate New York. She had grown apprehensive even before her husband, a sales manager for a California Internet firm and the father of a three-month-old daughter, called and confirmed her worst fears: "There are bad people on the plane." Jeremy Glick had heard the incoming reports and

rumors, and now said, "I need to know, are they crashing planes into the World Trade Center?" Lyz considered for a moment, surmising what her husband might do with the information, then told him that, yes, it was true. "Do you think we should attack the hijackers?" Glick asked his wife, indicating that there had already been some talk. She didn't know what to say, and then she did: "You do what you have to do, Jeremy. Be brave."

Jeremy Glick was on an Airfone, and so was Todd Beamer. "I know I'm not going to get out of this," the sales account manager for Oracle, who lived in Cranbury, N.J., told Lisa Jefferson, a GTE Airfone operator. He asked her to pray with him and told her that some passengers might make a run at the hijackers. At one point the father of two, whose wife—now widow—is due in January, said, absently, "Lisa."

"Yes," said Jefferson.

"Oh, that's my wife's name. I would like you to call her if I don't make it through this."

"That's my name, too, Todd."

"Oh, God."

Mark Bingham, head of his own bicoastal PR firm, called his mother, Alice Hoglan, in Saratoga, Calif. This was not to seek or disseminate critical information; Bingham knew what was happening, and what might happen next. "I want to tell you I love you," he said.

The four men were all in their thirties and were all athletic. Bingham, a six-foot-five surfer and rugby player, had ridden the horns of a bull this summer in Pamplona, Spain, and lived to tell about it. The publicly gay San Franciscan had once wrestled a gun from a mugger's hand, then beat up the mugger and his accomplice. He was tough as nails, and so was Glick, six foot two, burly and skilled. At the University of Rochester (N.Y.) in 1993, he was the national collegiate judo champ in the 220-pound division. Beamer had been an infielder for the Wheaton (Ill.) College baseball team, and Burnett had been a star quarterback for Jefferson High's football team in Bloomington, Minn. This gang of four was the hijackers' worst nightmare.

Jefferson, the GTE operator, said the Lord's Prayer with Beamer, then promised him that she would call his wife and tell her of their conversation, should things not turn out right. She heard Beamer ask someone, "Are you ready?" then heard him say, "Okay, let's roll." "Let's roll" was a favorite catchphrase in the Beamer household; three-year-old David used it all the time, as did his parents.

We know that the fight to take back the plane did not last long, and again we know it from the phone calls: Jefferson hung on the line for 15 minutes waiting for word from Beamer, but heard nothing more. The final words Jeremy Glick spoke to Lyz were, "I love you. Hold on to the phone and I'll be back." Lyz couldn't bring herself to listen. Her father, Richard Makely, took the receiver, then held his daughter close. He heard a minute of quiet, then screams, another moment of calm, more screams, then silence. He kept the phone to his ear for a painfully long time—more than an hour—hoping against hope.

The Boeing 757, which much earlier had made a hard turn over Ohio, signaling the more alert passengers that something—besides the hijacking itself—was not right, roared low over the Pennsylvania countryside, startling a caddie master who was on the grounds of the Laurel Valley Golf Club in Ligonier, Pa. He watched as the jet disappeared over the horizon. He saw it start to wobble just before it was out of sight. About three minutes later, at 10 a.m., it crashed in Shanksville, killing all 45 aboard. The hijackers' mission—the Capitol? the White House?—had been foiled.

Tom Burnett had a personal motto: Everybody else first, me second. It speaks for the four of them, and any others aboard Flight 93 who determined to take back the plane, take back their own fate, take away the murderous intent of the terrorists. They saved many lives, on a day of wanton killing.

Guiding influences in Bingham's life included grandmother Betty Hoglan (with Mark, right) and mother Alice, below.

Aboard Flight 11

Passengers were able to wrest their fate from the hijackers of Flight 93. No such option was possible aboard American Flight 11 out of Boston, the first plane to smash into the World Trade Center. Nevertheless, there was valiant behavior upon that plane, as senior flight attendant Madeline Amy Sweeney of Acton, Mass., kept her wits and realized that the passage of information was crucial in a situation such as this.

She made two calls from the plane's galley on one of the in-flight phones. She called her husband, Matthew, and she called control back at Boston's Logan International Airport. Ground supervisor Michael Woodward took that call, and listened as Sweeney talked with eerie calm about what had happened, and what was happening. She described the hijackers and detailed how they had killed a passenger and attacked two other flight attendants. She gave their seat locations, which allowed authorities to ascertain early on who might be culpable, and who—beyond the planes—needed to be watched. Her brother-in-law Bob Sweeney, a former professional hockey player with the Boston Bruins, said later: "The call she made from the flight provided valuable information to the FBI and was instrumental in identifying the hijackers. In the most difficult circumstances, she stayed calm. She did her job. Of course she tried to help. Helping was like breathing to her."

She stayed on the telephone with Woodward until the very end. She told him that she saw the Hudson River and, then, the Twin Towers. She said that the plane was flying low, too low. Reported Bob Sweeney: "She took a deep breath and very calmly spoke the words 'Oh, my God' one time. Not in fear, but in her own amazement."

Last Rites

Father Mychal Judge was approached at the St. Francis of Assisi Friary in Manhattan where he lived and told, simply, "I think they need you." Such a message rarely meant good news, for Judge, 68, was chaplain of the New York Fire Department. When they needed him quickly, it often had to do with death or distress. Father Judge put on his uniform and rushed across the street to the Engine 1 and Ladder 24 firehouse, where he spent a lot of time, shared many meals. He rode downtown with two of his men.

Ed Betz/AP

Father Mike, invoking the victims of TWA Flight 800 who died in Long Island Sound, once said, "Open your hearts, and let their spirit and life keep you going."

on to his 300th patient, the security guard standing his post to keep the flow of evacuees moving, the Red Cross volunteer in his or her 24th hour at the blood bank. The police and firefighters, of course. The priest giving last rites. Those who knew him aver that Father Judge would agree with the notion and would say that it was merely his work—God's work—being done, and there was nothing heroic about it. He would go on to point out that there are many tasks to a chaplaincy. But as he enumerated them, it would become apparent: His was a vocation for a hero.

Father Judge's work was everywhere, it was constant, and it was ecumenical, spreading across all lines of race, social status and faith. A Brooklyn-born son of Irish immigrants, his daily mission involved not only firemen but New York's homeless, immigrants, prisoners, AIDS sufferers, addicts. "He was a priest for all people," his friend and colleague at St. Francis, Father Brian Jordan, remembered. He had done work not dissimilar to that of September 11 before: After TWA Flight 800 crashed in Long Island Sound in 1996, Judge stayed for weeks at a Ramada Inn that had become a center for grieving families. He consoled people of many different religions—some of no religion at all—and stayed in touch with most until his death. Father Judge had recently accompanied a police-officer friend to Northern Ireland on a peace effort.

His mission was widespread, but his fellow friars and the firefighters were his family, his home. He had married many of the men and women in the department and had baptized their children. He had laughed with them—often—and counseled them in times of despair. They came en masse to his funeral at St. Francis on September 15, some in crisp dress uniform and others caked with sweat and grime, straight from the rubble where they were still searching, in vain, for survivors. In his homily, the Reverend Michael Duffy recalled a conversation with the chaplain. "Do you know what I need?" Mychal Judge had once asked Father Duffy. "Absolutely nothing. Why am I so blessed?"

It was noted often that day that Father Judge had been the first official victim of the attack. One firefighter had a lovely theory: "I just think God wanted somebody to lead the guys to heaven."

The story of Judge's death early in the action of September 11, told so many times that it already has the sheen of legend, is breathtaking in its poignancy. The friar had removed his helmet and knelt by a firefighter to give last rites when debris struck him in the head. Father Judge's comrades carried their fallen spiritual leader in a chair to St. Peter's Church, where his remains were placed in the sanctuary. Later, they were taken to his firehouse, thence to his friary.

It has been said of some of the day's heroes—and they would surely say it of themselves—that they were just doing their jobs. The doctor moving

Six Men and a Lady

They're now called the Lucky Six. On a day when many of their brothers died in burning buildings, six brave firemen from Ladder Company 6 proved that miracles still happen. The big guys were saviors, and were saved in return—by a little old lady (well, not that old). Theirs was a rare happy story that heartened grief-stricken New Yorkers.

Their station house was in Chinatown, on Canal Street. Normally they worked tenements, not skyscrapers. On the morning the towers came down, however, everything changed. Five of the six were on duty, while one was getting ready to go home. They heard the boom, then the intercom: "A plane just hit the World Trade Center."

Within minutes they were at the Center, rushing through the lobby of the north tower even as the second plane was bearing down on the south.

No elevators were running; the men headed for Stairway B, throwing on gear as they went. Each carried more than a hundred pounds. As they climbed, they met people coming down who handed them water from the vending machines. They reached the 12th floor, stopped to catch their breath, then struggled onward.

By the 27th floor they saw no more evacuees. Just then, a tremendous rumble told them that the south tower had just collapsed. "If that building can go, this building can go," said Capt. John Jonas, leader of the intrepid if desolate band. "It's time to head down."

Halfway back to earth, they met Josephine Harris, a grandmother from Brooklyn. She had walked down from her 73rd-floor office at the Port Authority and was exhausted, scared, not walking very well. The men hadn't expected to stop, but surely they could not abandon her. One of them wrapped

The Lucky Six and their lucky charm, from left: Firefighters Matt Komorowski, Tommy Falco and Sal D'Agostino; Harris; Captain Jonas; Firefighters Bill Butler and Mike Meldrum. Opposite: Butler's helmet—and the man himself—went through hell that day.

her arms around his neck, and they resumed their descent. Progress was excruciatingly slow since they could go no faster than assisting Harris would allow. It was a race against time, but they were determined to stick together. On the fourth-floor landing, her legs finally gave out. She said she could not go on. That's when the north tower disintegrated. "Everything starts heaving," recalled Captain Jonas to *The New York Times*. "Unbelievable noise. Everything flying around. Tremendous dust clouds. I'm thinking, 'I can't believe this is how it ends for me.'" All six— plus one—expected to die.

For a period, everything was chaos and calamity, as they were hurled about and the world came down around them. Then the wreckage settled, and they were in it. The stairwells were blocked; there was no way out. They pried open what had been the second-floor door.

All they could see was debris. But, suddenly, there: For whatever providential reason, a two-floor section of stairway had remained intact, and it

became their ladder to salvation. The men placed a harness around Harris, who was thoroughly covered in dust and grime, and slid her down. Then there was nothing to do but sit and wait. After several hours, the air began to clear and a beam of sunlight shone on them.

Once they were liberated, the firemen radioed for help, and two ladder companies responded. Harris was taken out in a basket. All seven got out alive. Had they been going a little faster—at the firemen's pace—they would have dropped below the second floor, perhaps to the lobby. Had they been slower—Harris's pace—they would still have been above the fifth floor, where the stairway was severed. Every mass tragedy has a story, or seven of them, like this. At the World Trade Center there were too few.

The next day, Harris was able to visit the Canal Street firehouse. The Lucky Six proudly presented her with a green fire jacket that was inscribed JOSEPHINE, OUR GUARDIAN ANGEL.

Fred R. Conrad/The New York Times

Desperate to Do More

By 10 a.m., only an hour after the second plane had hit the World Trade Center, Dr. Roger Yurt and the staff of the Weill Cornell Burn Center of New York Presbyterian Hospital were prepared for a huge number of wounded. Theirs is widely renowned as the best burn unit in the entire country, and it seemed inevitable that, at any moment, a flood of patients would be rushed up the East Side of Manhattan to the clinic. Yurt was confident he could handle the flood; he was encouraged by how his people had already responded. "We have a standard disaster plan, which includes calling in staff that aren't on duty," he said, "but we didn't have to do that. When they heard the news, our staff just came." Forty beds stood ready, and plans were in place to handle the overflow. "We were anticipating about a hundred."

The Center performed admirably, though the flood never came. In all, Weill Cornell received 25 patients; this was an early indication of how overwhelmingly fatal the collapse of the towers had been. Doctors at St. Vincent's Hospital in Greenwich Village, at the triage center set up on the West Side and elsewhere throughout the city were experiencing the same sad realization as Yurt: The early influx of patients was being followed not by inundation but by a slowing flow. "We were hoping for more than we received," he said simply, as he recalled the attack three weeks later.

Twenty-five patients in a burn unit is still a considerable number, and the level of intensity at the center in the aftermath of the attack was extreme. Yurt didn't return to his home in Ramsey, N.J., until late in the week. Working 38 hours straight with only a single two-hour pause for a nap, he had a part in treating 21 patients. Many of them were

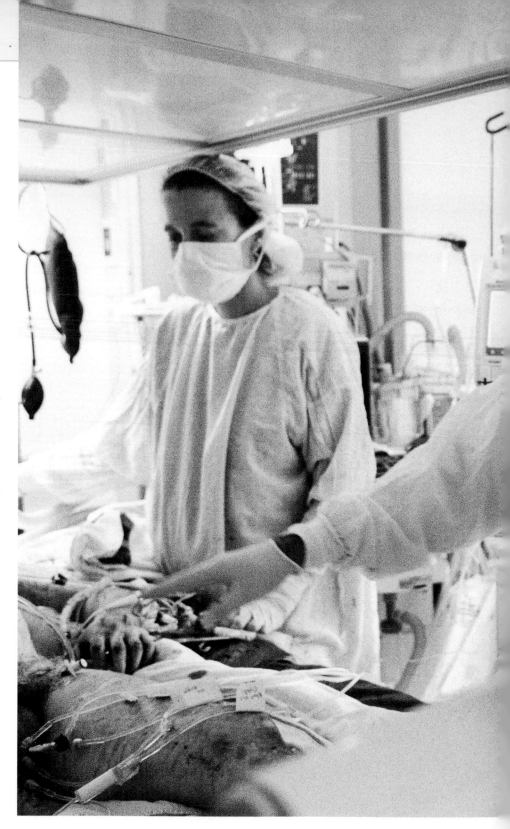

burned over 40 to 80 percent of their bodies. "Some had been burned near the scene of the crashes and others had been near elevators, either in the lobby or up higher," said Yurt. "Those patients described fireballs coming out of the elevator doors at several locations."

One victim died on arrival, and three of the

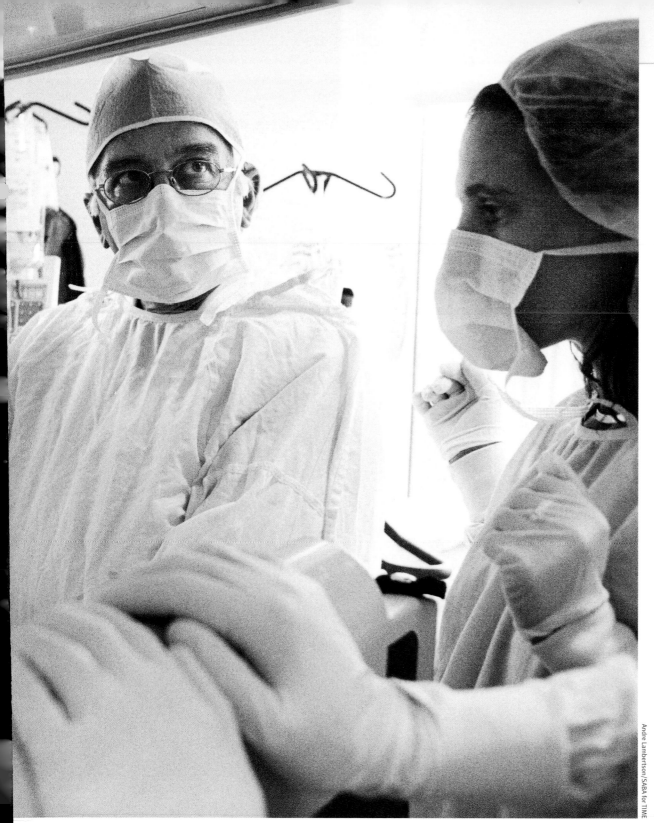

On the horrible day, Dr. Yurt treated a patient who had serious burns over 80 percent of his body. No surgery was possible until normal blood pressure could be maintained.

most critically injured succumbed in the weeks following the attacks. Only a quarter of the most severely burned are expected to survive, but there have been inspiring victories. "Our first critical patient was released from the hospital three weeks after the attacks," said Yurt. "He had had 35 percent of his body burned, half with third-degree burns and half with second-degree." The man's recovery was speedy, Yurt says, because he exhibited an extraordinary motivation to get out of bed and back to his life. "That makes a big difference," said Yurt, who might have been speaking of so many other kinds of victims of September 11, as well as his burn patients.

Her traumatic journey behind her, Hansen welcomed a hug from Benfante, one of her gallant benefactors.

Twin Moments of Truth

It is a potent human moment, when a critical decision must instantly be made. The wrong move can destroy a life; the right move can save one. You're fleeing imminent danger, and you see another person in dire jeopardy. Do you save yourself? The impulse must be irresistible. It is a telling moment.

Both Michael Benfante and John Cerqueira lived that moment, and each learned something about himself. Benfante, 36, and Cerqueira, 22, worked for the telecommunications firm Network Plus on the 81st floor of the north tower. On September 11, suddenly, "No one knew what had happened," said Benfante. "I saw flames flickering to the side of the building and could feel the whole thing swaying." Along with their colleagues, they began to dash down the stairs.

On the 68th floor, the two men were brought to a halt. Ahead of them, behind glass doors, 41-year-old Tina Hansen, a marketing supervisor at the Port Authority, was sitting helpless and distraught. A folded-up wheelchair nearby instantly told the story. The men hurried in, and while they struggled to open the wheelchair—a special light one for emergencies that she had gotten after the '93 Trade Center bombing—she begged them to

take her $8,000 motorized chair. "It was heavy," said Benfante. "There was no way." They strapped her into the lighter chair and set off on their trek.

Benfante is five eleven, 175 pounds. Cerqueira is the same height, with another 25 pounds. Benfante's experience as a football player at Brown brought strength and endurance into play. Cerqueira's years as an altar boy provided something else.

The way was arduous, often through acrid smoke. "In the back of my head, I could hear my mother telling me to get the heck out of there," said Cerqueira, "but I had to help." At one point, they were in total darkness and the floor was flooded from sprinklers. "It was like being in *The Poseidon Adventure,*" said Benfante, adding that Hansen stayed brave throughout. "I wasn't going out unless she was with me."

The rescue mission took more than an hour, but when they got to the bottom, an emergency van was there to take Hansen to safety. After a moment, Benfante and Cerqueira looked up and discovered that the south tower had disappeared, then they became aware that their tower was about to collapse. Finally, it was time to think of themselves, and the two office workers, who stood tall for someone who couldn't, found their own safety.

The Bravest

Just days after the attack, a couple walking on 51st Street in midtown Manhattan carried a number of shopping bags and a box too bulky for a bag. The box had big letters saying EMERGENCY RESCUE FIRETRUCK and see-through panels that revealed a gleaming red vehicle within.

The toy was surely bound for some youngster who, like any other, needed heroes to worship, perhaps to emulate. Now a new heroic breed had vaulted into a pantheon that only yesterday seemed reserved for athletes and rock stars. Of course, firefighters had been American heroes for a very long time, but with the advent of movies and television, there were other, flashier heroes to vie for the heart. Then, in one day, we were reminded of the promise made by these real-world saviors to sacrifice themselves on any given morning just as a matter of course. To be so instructed in the ethos of their valor was, for many Americans, humbling.

In a day smitten with heroics, the firefighters emerged—in the face of stiff competition—as the superheroes of September 11. And although George Washington did not "win" the Revolutionary War, although Ike did not "win" World War II, still their leadership must be credited with providing the example, with showing the right way to act. In the manner of leadership, none surpassed Peter J. Ganci, the chief of the New York City Fire Department—and he must stand here, as he did on that day, for all of his men.

A 33-year veteran, Ganci was in charge of all 11,550 uniformed personnel, as well as the Bureau of Emergency Medical Services. But this wasn't a general who led from a distant safe haven. As one of his colleagues said, "He had real down-the-long-hallway-and-take-people-out-of-burning-buildings medals."

Ganci, who had wanted to be a firefighter since he was 16 years old, was at Ground Zero minutes after the first plane hit the north tower. He established a command center there and spoke briefly with Mayor Giuliani. Ganci was working his multichannel radio when he sensed amid the chaos that the building wasn't stable. He immediately ordered his men to evacuate, thereby saving many lives. Knowing, however, that scores of his people were still inside, he chose to go after them. His deputy, Daniel Nigro, said, "He went directly back into harm's way in the most dangerous situation you've ever seen. It's important for the country to know that."

The crumbling tower claimed the life of the 54-year-old fire chief, and so many of his beloved firefighters. "He wouldn't tell you he was a five-star chief," said Ganci's son Chris. "He would say, 'I'm a New York City fireman.'"

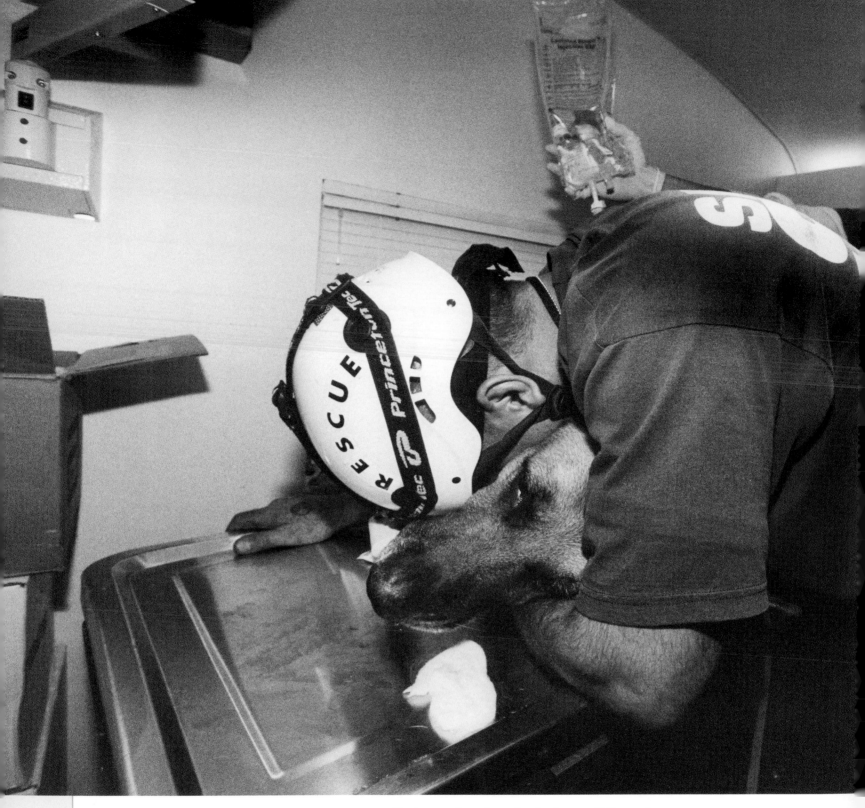

Man's Best Friends

There was another group of rescuers, some 300 strong, who pawed their way over mountains of concrete and metal, burrowed through voids and sniffed for survivors. The K-9 rescue dogs came with their handlers from around the world and, by nightfall on September 11, were searching franti-cally. It was thought to be the largest K-9 search effort ever, and one of the toughest.

"They had us staging out of a high school audi-torium nearby," remembered Fred Golba of Chicopee, Mass., owner of Amo, an 8-year-old Ger-man shepherd who has traveled with him to Cen-tral and South America and India for search-and-rescue missions. "We were working by 6:15 that

Harry Benson

Rescue dogs are trained to pick up human scent—their powerful noses can detect it through concrete—so, in the beginning, there was great expectation, and every hit was a hopeful one. "Once a dog gave its signal, the firefighters would come over and dig like a hungry rottweiler because they thought one of their fallen brothers would be down there," said Golba.

Certainly—faithfully—the dogs did all they were asked to do. Some rode over smoldering rubble in a basket-and-pulley system to get to their search areas; others went underground wearing cameras to give rescuers a subterranean view. Some of the dogs had been trained only to find survivors, and their hearts broke, along with those of their

After Amo's incident on the girder, he was given painkillers and an I.V. Below: Ricky the terrier, handled by Janet Linker of FEMA's Urban Search and Rescue division, worked the 7-to-7 night shift.

Andrea Booher/FEMA

evening, and didn't come back for 86 hours. Amo slept for three days after that."

Like the medics treating the human rescuers, volunteer veterinarians were on hand to care for the working canines. "Amo had three I.V.s, and he got antibiotics and pain medication for a time when he fell off a girder," said Golba. "I lost track of the number of times he had his eyes washed out."

On September 21, a German shepherd with a French search team worked the rubble. On the 23rd, Britany, a golden retriever, took a well-earned nap. Opposite: Hingson and his yellow Lab, Roselle, outside the family home in Westfield, N.J. When they go in, Roselle's harness comes off and her work is done— she's free to be a dog.

Andrea Booher /FEMA (2)

human counterparts, when their efforts proved fruitless. To raise spirits, some handlers would ask a volunteer to lie in a safe area of rubble or under a blanket so their dog could end its shift by "saving" someone. These feigned rescues did indeed bolster spirits all around, if only temporarily.

For dogs like Amo, who was trained to find humans alive or dead, the scene at Ground Zero was business as usual. He searched several 100-square-foot grids, and after four days, the end of his duty, he had built an impressive but gruesome record: the complete or partial remains of 44 separate bodies found. "Of course it's very hard to deal with," said Golba, weeks after the attack. "But I went in, did my job, cried about it, and then it was over. Amo works for praise, so he was working hard and loving his job. He had plenty of appreciation, not just from me, but from firefighters who came up to hug him and pet him and tell him he's a good dog." Then Golba paused, nothing left to say.

The search-and-rescue dogs provided only half the canine story. On September 11, on the 78th floor of the north tower, Michael Hingson, who is blind, was preparing for a meeting when the first attack plane struck. His three-year-old Labrador, Roselle, hurried to his side. "She knew something was different," said Hingson. "But she never freaked out and never lost her focus." Guide dogs

James Salzano

train for more than a year in stressful situations, where loud noises like gunshots are used to distract them; only the strongest graduate. "I held on to Roselle with my left hand and the rail with my right, like I usually do when going down stairs," recalled Hingson, who was also assisted by his colleague David Frank. "People were talking, some were nervous and breathing rapidly." At about the

25th floor, someone was handing out bottles of water, and Frank, Hingson and Roselle, who was panting heavily, stopped for a drink. An hour after the first plane hit, the group made it to daylight. "It's a team effort," said Hingson, weeks later. "Roselle and I rely on each other."

The dogs sensed some of what was going on, hardly most of it. They were luckier than they knew.

James Salzano

Protecting the Children

The 1995 bombing of the Oklahoma City federal building, in which 19 children were killed, still casts a shadow in this country, and when buildings were attacked on September 11, an immediate question was: Were there kids? Were there childcare centers?

There were. But there are other legacies of Oklahoma City than the shadow, and one of them helped protect the children. Since 1995 many child-care centers have spent much time and money to improve their security and emergency procedures. When New York and Washington were attacked, teachers knew exactly what to do. Of course, plans are only plans. That the teachers never flinched in the midst of the horror says as much about them as it does about safeguards and precautions.

Soon after the first plane slammed into the

World Trade Center, 14 teachers and the director of the Children's Discovery Center, Charlene Melville, had to evacuate their 28 charges, who ranged in age from four months to four and a half years old. Adhering to the drill they practiced every month, they gathered up emergency records for each, picked up the babies, traveled down from the second floor and herded everyone outside. In their rush to leave Building No. 5, which later collapsed, purses and even shoes were left behind. Once outside, they paused to rest on the steps of a nearby church. "White smoke was billowing out of the top of the tower," Melville remembered later. "But we thought it would be put out, and that we would be back the next day." But then they heard the impact of the second plane and knew they had to get away, and fast. "People yelled. Everyone was scared." When the first tower collapsed, the teachers headed north, away from the flying debris. "We grabbed the kids and started to run. We were able to stay ahead of the dust cloud all the way." The teachers tried to stay together but eventually were split into two groups by the pressing throng. One group commandeered shopping carts at a nearby grocery store and filled them with preschoolers. They pushed farther north.

With babies perched on their hips, the caretakers tried to call parents on borrowed cell phones. Melville showed such presence of mind that, at Pace University, she stopped to place three important calls. She got in touch with corporate headquarters to let them know the children were safe; she called the childcare center and put the same message on the answering machine in anticipation of anxious parents; and she phoned local TV stations and asked them to broadcast her destination so parents would know where to pick up their kids.

That destination was St. Vincent's Hospital in Greenwich Village. The other group went to a school, where Melville tracked them down. All the children were safely reunited with parents by 3:45. Melville retained her focus throughout. "I would not allow myself to feel anything until I got home, then it hit me." She added: "I felt I had the angels with me that day, and that God was leading me."

Meanwhile, in Washington, the Children's World Learning Center near the Pentagon had to

be evacuated after Flight 77 struck. Director Shirley Allen, a 12-year veteran in early childhood education, thought only about the safety of her 140 charges, ranging in age from eight weeks to five years, even though her husband was at work in the Pentagon. Allen and her 36 colleagues also followed the drills they practiced monthly. They collected the children, put the babies into movable cribs and, accompanied by two helpers from the building, headed for a nearby park. "Moving 12 cribs over the bumpy grounds was hard work, but many strangers stopped to help," remembered Allen a month later. The group had to be relocated five times by rescue workers. Allen insisted that security police stay with them.

The teachers played patty-cake and sang "Eensy Weensy Spider" to draw attention away from the chaos that surrounded them. "The children were relaxed because they looked into their teachers' faces and saw they were relaxed," Allen said. "It was a big team effort. It was truly a united America that day." Three hours after the ordeal had begun, most of the parents were back with their youngsters. Only then did Allen permit herself to worry about her husband. He was safe. But when all the counting had been done and all the kids were in the hands of guardians, it became evident that two of them had lost a parent.

A month after the attacks, Melville (opposite) was smiling again, and Allen revisited the bridge across which she marched her brigade of preschoolers.

Courtesy of Nicole De Martini

Frank's Tower

Frank loved his job and the building where he worked, but above all he loved his homelife with Nicole and the children.

They usually went to work separately. But not on the morning of September 11. On that day, Frank and Nicole De Martini dropped their children off at school and drove to the Twin Towers together. They arrived early and Frank invited his wife to come up to his office for a cup of coffee.

Frank, 49, was construction manager of the World Trade Center. An architect by trade, his association with the Twin Towers dated to 1993 when, following the terrorist bombing that year, he was hired to assess damage and help with the repairs. His office was on the 88th floor of Tower No. 1, several stories up from his wife's. Nicole, 42, also an architect, had close ties to the great buildings as well. A native of Switzerland, she had come to the United States at age 19 to study architecture at Pratt Institute in Brooklyn. Employed by the engineering firm that erected the towers, she worked with a team that inspected their structural integrity every year.

The De Martinis arrived at Frank's office at about 8:15. A half hour later, Nicole was about to head back to her floor when the plane struck. "The building shook a little, then stabilized quickly," she recalled several weeks later. "Huge flames were shooting outside. The room quickly filled with smoke." The couple thought a bomb had detonated. They remained calm, in part because, as experts, they were aware of the building's extraordinary structural resilience.

Frank found a room that was relatively free of smoke for his wife and two dozen others, then went to look for a safe way down. He returned shortly, saying that he had found an open staircase. The evacuees needed to climb over a big pile of rubble to reach the stairwell. Frank helped each one get over. Then he hesitated. "Frank was behind me and I asked him to stay with me," Nicole remembered. But, suddenly, she had lost him amidst the crowd. She would later learn that her husband had stayed behind to help others on his floor. At one point Frank phoned his sister, Nina, to assure her that he and Nicole were safe.

Nicole walked down the steps through waves of dense smoke. On the 78th floor she passed an elevator that had passengers trapped inside. Someone was frantically trying to pry open the door.

Nicole's group was forced to switch stairways twice when traffic made movement impossible. Finally she reached the street. Her escape had taken 40 minutes.

Exhausted, Nicole headed to her home, and children, in the Fort Greene section of Brooklyn. "My whole thought was on my kids." Sabrina, 10, and Dominic, eight—were unaware of their parents' fate. Nicole was nearing the Brooklyn Bridge when Tower No. 2—the other tower, not Frank's tower—collapsed. She and hundreds of others also heading toward the bridge were engulfed in a swirl of dust; life had become unreal. Shortly thereafter, World Trade Center Tower No. 1 crumbled.

Nicole did not reach home until six that night. By then she knew that she would never see her husband again. She wondered how many people he helped over the rubble. She wondered if, perhaps, he reached the 78th floor and—perhaps—freed those people from the elevator. She knows for certain only what she tells her children: that their father had died helping other people to safety.

All-American Volunteers

The recovery effort was, of course, staggering. Firemen, police officers, FBI agents and thousands of other workers needed strength and sustenance as they grappled with the horror and grief of each day. In New York and Washington, countless generous people pitched in to provide whatever they could. A few blocks from Ground Zero in Manhattan, Nicole Blackman worked around the clock handing out steaming cups of coffee. Drew Nieporent owned six restaurants in the area. When they were shut down after the attack, he fed workers instead of paying customers. Some of New York's choicest eateries sent gourmet takeout.

In Washington the attack on the Pentagon brought together Mohammed Tabibi, 20, an Afghani American, and Gail Batt, 54, a volunteer police counselor.

Tabibi is the only child of Afghani immigrants who have lived in this country close to 25 years. He attended public schools in Arlington, Va., and became interested in police work when he was a high school junior. He signed up as a student intern at the local police station and has been working there ever since. On the morning of the attack, his father was driving a taxi near the Pentagon and saw the plane hit. His mother was at her office but left at noon and headed home, where Mohammed was preparing to go to the police station. "I pleaded with him to stay," she said in an interview weeks after the attack, "You are my only child." Mohammed replied: "I must go, Mom. They need me right now. You must respect my decision."

When he arrived at the station he ran into Gail Batt. A volunteer for the Arlington Police Department for nearly four years, Batt's principal assignment was to counsel crime victims. Last year she was named one of the outstanding volunteers of Arlington County for her work with the police. She too had heard the plane crash, just after she had dropped her daughter off at the subway stop in the Pentagon. She had spent anxious moments, then learned her daughter was safe. Now there was only

Batt (with bottles) and Tabibi reviewed plans for their relief efforts with officers at the Arlington, Va., police station where both were affiliated.

Tyrone Turner/Black Star

one place to go: the police station.

At around one p.m. she and Tabibi went to a back room to fill bags with sandwiches for police officers. There was a photo of Osama bin Laden on the wall, and one of the workers turned to Tabibi and said, "You're from Afghanistan, aren't you?" He looked up with tears in his eyes and replied: "I'm an American. I was born in this country. I love this country. We didn't do this."

When they ran out of food, Batt decided to go begging. She and Tabibi went to the Fresh Fields market, which had already closed. They knocked on the door. The manager loaded up their carts, even though she had already supplied the Red Cross. The response was strong elsewhere as well: Bountiful free food was supplied by supermarkets, delis and deluxe restaurants. Batt pulled up to the Four Seasons Hotel in downtown Washington in a police van and filled it with gourmet meals.

Tabibi stayed at the station for six hours the first day, then was put to work for a week doing odd jobs for some of the officers. "I did whatever I could to make their job easier," said Tabibi. Batt, too, put in long hours at the station house during subsequent weeks. "This small effort is just a way to put my arms around the victims and say 'I'm here,'" she said, calling it "a privilege to be part of the whole experience."

Tabibi and Batt are no more nor less worthy than the thousands of others who helped in Washington and New York, but the dynamic at the heart of this duo, who were thrown together by the cataclysm, makes them a perfect symbol for an American generosity of spirit on display that awful day. To reiterate: Batt was a volunteer at the police station well before September 11; it is in her bones to volunteer, it is instinct. Tabibi's parents came to the United States from Afghanistan with one thought in mind—a better life. Mohammed is currently working another job besides the one at the police station to put himself through college. Tabibi and Batt's is a story of native and immigrant Americans, and how the pull of patriotism in this country is so strong, so irresistible. Tabibi, for his part, worries about family members in Afghanistan, but hopes that the Taliban will be destroyed. "That is one good thing that will come of this."

The Lieutenant's Clinic

The Horohos, both colonels in the Army, thanked neighbor Kelly Spencer for taking care of Maggie, seven, as Maggie's friend Breana Kiernan looked on.

One of the immediate tasks facing survivors of the September 11 attack was to help the wounded, to ease their pain and suffering, to keep them alive. Victims with severe burns, cuts, broken bones, smoke inhalation and trauma needed treatment the minute they escaped from the flaming buildings.

At the Pentagon no one was quicker to respond than Lt. Col. Patty Horoho, 41. An Army health-policy officer, she had been in the service for 18 years. That morning she was in her office watching the Trade Tower disaster. "I knew that there would be a series of attacks, and that we would be next," she recalled later. "I walked across the hall and then it went boom." Flight 77 had just struck 100 yards away. Horoho, who had earlier in her career received training as a clinical nurse specializing in burn care and trauma, took charge. "I felt like my life and career had been a preparation for this moment," she said. "I truly believe that is why I could take charge."

She rushed outside to a grassy area close to a highway and began to set up a triage center. "Then God intervened. Someone drove by and tossed a medical aid bag with I.V.s and fluid over the guard rail," she said. She put the first evacuees to work.

Father Brian Jordan (second from left) returned to Ground Zero on October 4. The friend of the late Father Mychal Judge blessed a cross of steel beams that had been found amidst the rubble of Tower No. 1.

Kathy Willens/AP

Among them were a brigadier general and three sailors who had crawled out of the flames on their bellies. "They came up to me, their clothes ripped, their hair singed. They said, 'Can we help?' " She ordered them to cut clothing off the burn victims and set up I.V. bags. They used one of the men's belts as a tourniquet.

Soon, Horoho had a half dozen helpers. For four hours she focused on the 75 victims at her makeshift clinic. "She showed great resolve and courage," said Air Force Sgt. Noel Sepulveda, 51, a former medic of the Vietnam and Gulf wars, who worked close beside her during this time and provided specialized assistance. An EMS team arrived, as did many selfless people from all over the district. One pediatrician closed his practice to lend a hand. Then Dr. James Vafier, an emergency doctor from a nearby hospital, arrived on the scene, and headed up the medical operations. Only after six hours of concentrated effort did Horoho take the time to call her family. She reached her husband, Ray, and "got the warmest 'I love you' I've ever gotten," she said. A reservist with the Army, Ray was called to the Pentagon later in the day to help mobilize reserve soldiers.

Patty Horoho went back to work, and continued until 12:30 in the morning, when she finally had to retrieve her three children who were being cared for by neighbors. "She did a yeoman's job making sure that everything was done properly," said Dr. Vafier. "She was absolutely superb—organized and easy to work with."

Asked about this a month after the attack, Horoho, in character, demurred: "It was an integrated effort by so many people. I had never really thought about the name 'United States' before, but 'United' now has a very powerful meaning. I couldn't be more proud to be an American."

Postscript

And then there were the anonymous ones, the heroes who performed so many small and large acts automatically. We'll never know their names; we'll never be able to properly honor them. A firefighter remembers being lost in the rubble. He reached back and grabbed the arm of the next person and they started a chain, but now they were all lost together in the dark. Suddenly, the fireman was pulled forward, out of the twisted debris and into the light. By the time the several survivors got out, whoever had shown them the way was gone.

A woman in Washington lost her son in the attack on the Pentagon. Or was it her husband? Accounts differ, but the story is true. A week after the attack, she went to the neighborhood near the wounded building. She visited a Korean-run coffee shop near the cleanup site and gave the owner money along with instructions to use it to pay the bill of soldiers who were in that day. Later, an Air Force major came in, heard that his muffin was already paid for and was told the entire tale. "That poor woman should have been in deep mourning," he said. "Instead she's buying coffee and doughnuts for us guys in uniform. I have no answers to how someone cultivates a heart as large as that."

There are no answers for many of the events of September 11 and following. But with the acts of kindness, generosity, selflessness and heroism, at least, the mysteries are fine to contemplate.

LIFE asked Maya Angelou if she would write about heroes and heroism. She did, movingly.

Extravagant Spirits

by Maya Angelou

Without their fierce devotion
We are fragile and forlorn,
Stumbling briefly, among the stars.

We and our futures belong to them
Exquisitely, our beliefs and our
Breaths are made tangible in their love.

By their extravagant spirits, they draw us
From the safe borders
And into the center of the center ring
There they urge dance upon our
Leaden feet
And to our sullen hearts,
Bright laughter.

Not the crowd's roar nor the gasped
Breath of the timorous can stay their mission.

There is no moderation in their nature.
They spit upon their fingers
To test the wind of history,
They slip into our bonds and steal us
Away from the slavery of cowardice.

They skin back their thin lips over fanged teeth and
Rocks in hand, in our presence
Face down our Goliath.

These mothers, fathers, pastors and priests,
These Rabbis, Imams and gurus,
Teach us by their valor and mold us with their courage.

Without their fierce devotion
We are only forlorn and only fragile
Stumbling briefly, among the stars.

Christophe Agou for Newsweek

Faces of Ground Zero

There is an extraordinary camera in a studio in southern Manhattan, a 12-foot by 16-foot by 12-foot-high Polaroid. It is a one-of-a-kind instrument, designed in the 1970s at the behest of the visionary Edwin Land, who challenged his designers to make a camera as big as they could. It takes pictures that are 40 inches wide by 80 inches tall—larger than life-size—and yields images of striking immediacy and clarity. Its portraits reveal the person within.

Longtime LIFE photographer Joe McNally, architect of some of the biggest photographic productions ever attempted in the magazine industry, had used the camera, and when he saw what transpired at the World Trade Center, only blocks away from the studio, he felt that it would be worth the effort to create a document. Over the course of two weeks, nearly 150 people involved in the tragedy—survivors, firemen, policemen, volunteers, doctors, nurses, widows, children, desperate searchers in the rubble—came before McNally's

lens and, in a way, bared their souls. "I've been shooting through tears a lot," said McNally. "I've heard countless stories of heroism, loss and recovery. It's interesting—there hasn't been a single bitter or angry word. The mood in the studio has been one of acceptance and healing. Anger has been absent." McNally, at project's end, felt drained emotionally and physically, but convinced that the toil had been worthwhile, that his exhibit would stand as a dignified tribute to the courage displayed at Ground Zero. "I think this might be the one significant thing I will do as a photographer," said McNally, emphasizing that the victims of September 11 surely merit the tribute.

Nina Russo

Larry Olivetti 40
Officer, NYPD, Emergency Services Unit Truck 1

Olivetti worked in the Ground Zero search-and-rescue effort with "all sorts of tools," including shovels, a saw and an acetylene torch.

❝ I'd worked in building collapses before, but the buildings were three or four stories. Nothing like this. You hear all the clichés— that you have to be down there to understand the scale, that words can't describe it. Well, all the clichés are true. It took days for the reality of this thing to sink in. After a month, it still hasn't sunk in that our unit lost 14 guys. ❞

Billy Ryan 32
Mike Morrisey 47
Firefighters, Rescue 3

Each was home when the attack came, and got a call to come in. They arrived at the site just after the second collapse.

❝ I tried to get overtime the night before but signed up too late," said Morrisey. "It would have happened to me. Eight men in my 'house alone were killed, and I know of many more." Said Ryan: "Two tables of people at my wedding are not here anymore. I'm tired of burying my friends. ❞

Juana Lomi 37
Paramedic, NYU Downtown Hospital

She and her partner dashed to the scene. They survived the collapse of both towers, then they went to work.

❝ It was an overwhelming feeling of fear, horror—and not being able to do more. There were hundreds of people that needed to be treated. I was at risk of losing my life, but I had to stay and help other people. ❞

Manu Dhingra 27
**Securities Trader,
Andover Brokerage**

He was outside an elevator door on the 83rd floor of Tower No. 1 when the first plane hit. Burned over 40 percent of his body, he was rushed to the Weill Cornell Burn Unit.

On the way down, I really wanted to sit, but my co-workers lied to me: 'We're almost there.' People looked at me and grimaced. I thought, 'What kind of life am I walking down to?' But I'm the lucky one. I go back and visit the other patients, fighting for their lives, as often as I can. I hope to inspire them.

Donald T. Gromling 42
Timothy Hayes 34
Pilots, NYPD Aviation Unit

Theirs was the first helicopter on the scene after Tower No. 1 was hit.

We saw the second plane," said Gromling. "Peculiar. 'Where's this guy going?' He went right under our helicopter. His wings rocked three times, banking left and right. I prayed this was a bad dream. It impacted." Said Hayes: "I advised ground units to shut down airports, then continued to give reports about the conditions of the towers until they fell.

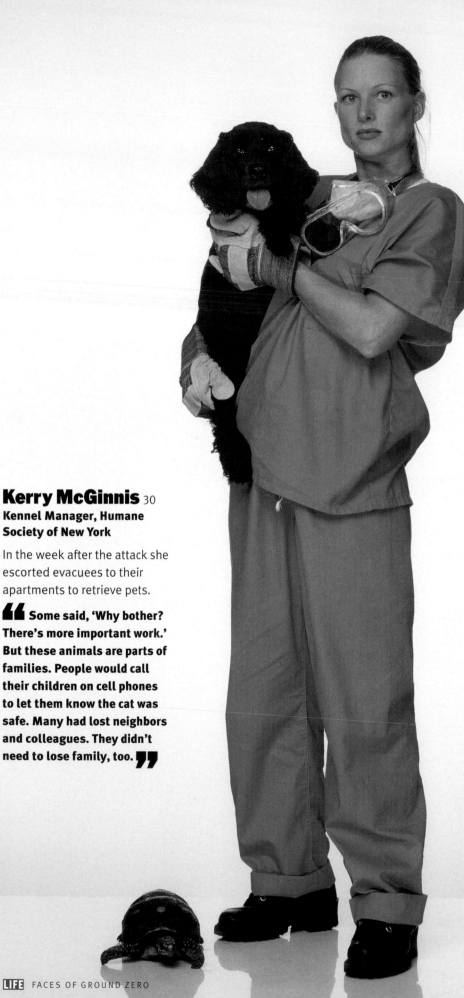

Kerry McGinnis 30
**Kennel Manager, Humane
Society of New York**

In the week after the attack she
escorted evacuees to their
apartments to retrieve pets.

**❝ Some said, 'Why bother?
There's more important work.'
But these animals are parts of
families. People would call
their children on cell phones
to let them know the cat was
safe. Many had lost neighbors
and colleagues. They didn't
need to lose family, too. ❞**

Bob LaRocco 46
Lieutenant, FDNY, Ladder 9

"Rocky" was off-duty on September
11 when the first plane struck, but
immediately headed back to his
firehouse. He had escaped from the
rubble of the first fallen tower when
the second came down.

**❝ As the collapse started to
outrun me, I dove behind a
firetruck. It's funny what you think,
your last thoughts. I actually
laughed, and I thought: 'Death,
I just cheated you and now you're
gonna come for the payoff.' ❞**

Archbishop Demetrios 73
**Archbishop of America,
Greek Orthodox Church**

Among the buildings destroyed was
St. Nicholas Greek Orthodox Church.

**" In the terrorist attacks we have
seen the abyss, the ugliness and
darkness of evil. In what followed
we have seen the immensity,
beauty and brilliance of good.
St. Nicholas will be rebuilt
on the exact same location,
but it will be much more
than a small parish church.
It will be a shrine, a
monument of remembrance,
a consecration of the
sacredness of life, a place
of reflection and peace
for anyone of any faith
or no faith. "**

Christopher Pepe 36
David Kravette 40
**Salesman and Managing
Director, Cantor Fitzgerald**

They were called from offices
on high just before the attack.

  The guy said he had to see
me, so I left Tower 1 at around
8:20 to go to Broad Street. That
call saved my life," said Pepe.
Said Kravette: "My assistant
was seven months pregnant, so
I offered to go down and meet
our guests. I was in the lobby
when it hit. No one from Cantor
Fitzgerald made it down.

Jan Demczur 48
Window Washer

When the plane struck Tower No. 1, Demczur and five others became trapped in an elevator 50 floors up. Demczur pried open the door with his squeegee. Faced with a wall of plasterboard, he went at it with the metal blade of his wiper. All of the trapped took turns and finally made a one-foot-by-18-inch hole. They crawled out, astonishing firefighters. The escape took 95 minutes.

❝ I can't talk about it. ❞

Elton Y. Kwok 17
Elliot Levy-Bencheton 16
Brendan Moore 17
Tayeb Al Karim 17
Elizabeth Alspector 15
Amanda Kwok 14
Students, Stuyvesant High School

Among 9,000 students in seven schools displaced by the attacks, they were lucky enough to be able to return to their school in mid-October.

❝ At first we didn't have school at all," said Alspector. "It felt like vacation, but with a giant cloud over it. If you look at Stuyvesant now, there are no signs that anything happened. But across the street there are army barracks. So unreal. Garbage trucks drive by carrying steel beams, rubble four blocks away. But it's good to be back. I feel safe here, like it's my home. ❞

Amanda Reno 21
Armando Reno 55
**Student;
Driver, FDNY, Engine 65**

Armando was putting out a car fire when the second tower collapsed. Firefighters worked all day to rescue him.

❝ I don't have any memory of it," said Armando. Said Amanda: "He always calls. We waited. Bellevue called and said he was stable. I felt like I was holding my breath six hours. I breathed again. ❞

Joseph Putkowski 45
Detective, NYC Bomb Squad

On vacation, he reported to the 6th Precinct on 10th Street.

" I was on a response team that covered packages coming into the city. I put on a bomb suit—75 layers of Kevlar with metal plates in front. I'm very saddened by the attack. I lost my best buddy, Claude Richards, who was evacuating people at the towers. The disaster brought me much, much closer to my family and friends. "

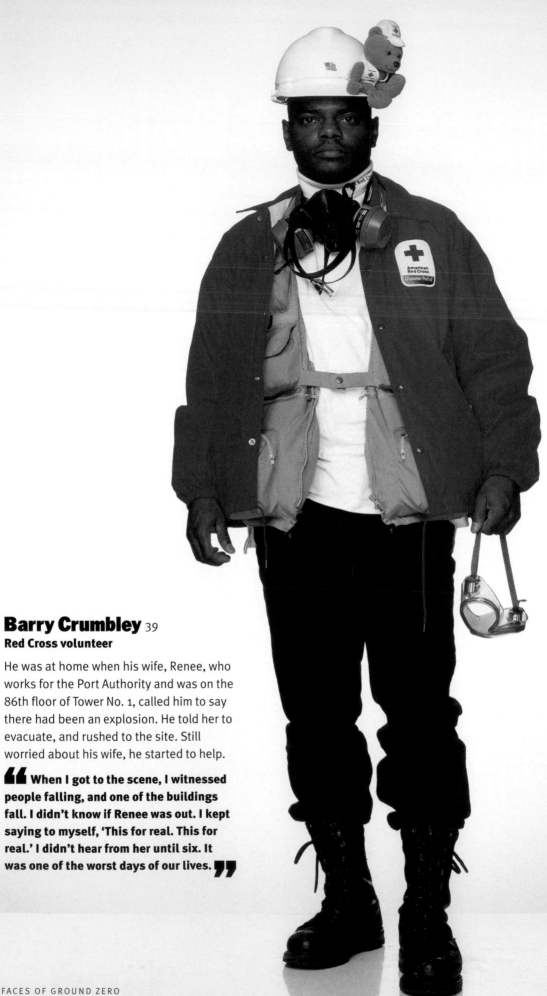

Barry Crumbley 39
Red Cross volunteer

He was at home when his wife, Renee, who works for the Port Authority and was on the 86th floor of Tower No. 1, called him to say there had been an explosion. He told her to evacuate, and rushed to the site. Still worried about his wife, he started to help.

❝ When I got to the scene, I witnessed people falling, and one of the buildings fall. I didn't know if Renee was out. I kept saying to myself, 'This for real. This for real.' I didn't hear from her until six. It was one of the worst days of our lives. ❞

Saade Mustafa 29
Television studio electrician

He was handing out food on Friday, September 14.

" An electrician knew me and said, 'Mustafa, grab your tool belt.' I ran cable and set up movie lights for the search. My parents are Palestinian. Islam is not terrorism. I was in the U.S. Navy in the Gulf war. Now there was a war at home. It was my duty as a human being—an American—and a New Yorker to be there. "

Rudolph W. Giuliani 57
Mayor of the City of New York

Hearing of the attack, he rushed
to the scene and took control.

**66 New Yorkers have conducted
themselves as bravely as people
did during the Battle of Britain.
In the 1940s they were bombed
every day, and still people went
about their living and showed
a great example of bravery and
courage to the rest of the world.
If we maintain a steady way
of life, we will be a great example
to the rest of the country and
the rest of the world. 99**

Louie Cacchioli 51
Firefighter, Engine 47

Rescued many from Tower No. 1

I stepped outside after bringing about 40 or 50 people down a stairway. I looked around. It was crazy. Somebody yelled, 'Look out! The tower's coming down!' I started running. I tossed my air mask away to make myself lighter. Next thing I know, there's a big black ball of smoke. I threw myself on my knees, and I'm crying. I said to myself, 'Oh, my God, I'm going to die.' I was crawling. Then—the biggest miracle thing in the world. My hands came onto an air mask. It still had air. Another 15 seconds, I wouldn't have made it.

Peter Regan 20
United States Marine

He was stationed at Camp Pendleton in California when the towers were hit and his father, Donald, a New York City firefighter with Rescue 3, rushed to the scene. Peter flew east and joined in recovery efforts at Ground Zero, searching for his dad.

❝ If the roles were reversed, I know he would do the same thing. I just want something of his. I would prefer to bring something back. ❞

Truskolaski Marek 35
Raul Pala 34
Julio Jalil 57
Asbestos handlers, Laborers International Union of North America, Local 78

They began cleanup efforts at Ground Zero on September 15.

❝ When I first got there, I was crying, thinking about the people who died and their families," said Marek. Said Pala: "This is so painful for anyone who is human." And Jalil: "When I saw it, I thought, It would take the devil to kill so many people. ❞

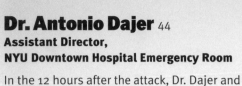

Dr. Antonio Dajer 44
Assistant Director,
NYU Downtown Hospital Emergency Room

In the 12 hours after the attack, Dr. Dajer and his staff treated 350 patients. Five died.

"You think you're ready for it, but it is much too fast. And when you see a woman, who was normal just 15 minutes earlier, come in with burns over her entire body, you just can't see any justification for it. You get a sense of how fragile and temporary life is. "

Katrina Marino 35
Wife of missing firefighter Kenneth Marino of Rescue 1, pictured with daughter Kristin, 3, and son Tyler, 1

Eleven firefighters from Rescue 1 responded to alarms. None returned.

❝ Kenny was listed as injured and I was very hopeful, but later they said it was a mistake. I try not to get upset in front of the kids. I need to be there for them. My daughter has been an inspiration. It came to the point where I had to tell her Daddy's in heaven. She said, 'Don't worry, Mommy, you've got me and Tyler.' ❞

Remembrance and Reflection

Asked how they felt on September 11 or thereafter, several very fine and very different writers from around the world shared their eloquent thoughts with LIFE. For some—a celebrated Australian novelist, a Washington news-bureau chief, a nonfiction writer in Atlanta who is the mother of five—the tragedy spurred reflections on family: their families and the family of man. For others—the son of an Iwo Jima flagraiser, the nation's preeminent biographer—the startling attack on New York and Washington prompted a search for historical context. For all, the effort to make sense of or find meaning in September 11 yielded reflections that are heartfelt, personal, poignant, often profound.

When I lived in Tribeca during the 1980s, I strolled the cobblestones of Greenwich Street many times. A quiet street of low-rise buildings, it was visually dead-ended by an immense gleaming tower, one of two. Walking down the street today though, there was no visual end to it. Just a sky-blue infinity with hazy smoke wafting skyward in the distance.

No cars are allowed—it is a street of mourners on foot now. Missing-person posters on your left and right like saints in stained glass mark your slow procession. Fernando was 56 and his smile produced a double chin. Alicia was single and posed with her poodle. Jaclyn's first job was on the 71st floor. She probably mailed that graduation photo along with her résumé. People returning from paying their respects walk up the lonely street toward you. Couples hold hands but they are not talking. Their eyes glance at store windows whose displays they do not see.

Then you are there. The wooden altar rail reads DO NOT CROSS; the altar boys are men in blue. About 40 people stand quietly gazing down the aisle-street at the squat pyre still smoldering after two hundred and eighty-eight hours. Murmured comments in English, French and Japanese waft over the crowd like prayers. The middle-aged guy in tennis shoes, shorts and a baseball cap is shaking his head. The sharp blonde in Gucci glasses begins to sob. The muscled policeman stands facing the crowd, thumbs tucked into his thick black leather belt. He hears our words, witnesses the grief. Dark glasses shield his eyes. I notice the corner of his mouth. It is twitching.

The rubble is somehow alive, somehow organic. It used to soar in orderly man-made lines. Now it is twisted haphazardly but naturally, like fallen trees in a forest, jumbled vines in the jungle. The smoke arising from the hulk seems to be paying respect to those within. It rises not in aggressive billows from a raging fire but calmly and lazily like incense outside a Buddhist temple.

It is an immense squashed mass still rising four or five stories, as squat and bulky as an old corner bank in a midsize American town. I imagine 200 people in that town's bank. Suddenly the bank implodes. Floors, walls, desks, chairs, ductwork, ceilings, cement, plastic, steel, computers, coffee cups and framed pictures of the kids crush them. Then 10, no 20 or more of these multistory banks fall upon the first. There will be no more arms or legs of dead sons and sisters found by the rescuers. Joyce and Joe are one with the rubble now.

Today the *New York Post* ran an article about the firemen who raised the flag above the rubble. I am quoted comparing their flagraising to my dad's on Iwo Jima; both flags from ships, both sets of flagraisers not aware of a nearby photographer, both shots offering hope.

As I look down Greenwich Street, I think of the comparative tolls of the Marine Corps' worst battle and America's worst civilian wound. The body count in southern Manhattan will approach the 6,824 white crosses and Stars of David planted on that Pacific isle. But there are differences. The 1945 black-and-white photo looks suddenly distant, last week's color shot up close and immediate. And everything moves so much more quickly now, the instant images, the round-the-clock coverage. The sudden collapse of the tall towers marks the compression of time in our modern age. As I turn from the memorial mound I think of the thousands of final screams in those last few fleeting seconds. In my father's long-ago time such tragedy took 36 long days.

—**James Bradley**, author of *Flags of Our Fathers*

I was a child in Romania when we gathered around our brand-new television to watch news of the assassination of John F. Kennedy. Nobody believed it. My uncle said that it was all fake, a plot by the Russians to destroy our minds. Television had barely come into being and it was strange enough to see the moving images. It was even stranger to see America for the first time. "Look at the amazing tall buildings," my mother said. They were amazing. The tall buildings. The energy of people moving fast even as they were weeping and mourning.

On September 11, 2001, the 21st century began in earnest. The whole world gathered around televisions to watch the horror visited upon us. My friend Ioana wrote from Romania that she had been watching with her son. She sent her heartfelt condolences and said, "We keep waiting for Bruce Willis to show up and for the movie to end!" I thought about her son Luca, who is the same age I was in 1963, and wondered what he was making of it. The tall buildings. The airplanes crashing into them. The flames. The people killed. This was his initiation into the new century, into how things really stand in history. The movie has no happy end. There is no Bruce Willis.

Amazingly, the Berlin Wall went down with little bloodshed, but the consequences were far from obvious at the time. We watched huge crowds bring down repressive governments peacefully (with the notable exception of Romania, where a moderately bloody "revolution" was staged for television). The repressive governments came down, leaving a power vacuum in their wake. All kinds of hungry ghosts came out of it, nationalism and fundamentalism among them. The United States, the only superpower left, became the natural target for all the haters of democracy, religious tolerance and the modern world in general.

Our belle epoque is over. We will look back on the '90s of the last century with the same nostalgia people looked back to the '90s of the 19th century. My sons, who were born within the golden bubble of the last quarter of the American century, have no idea. I wish they didn't have to.

Americans are not demonstrative people: We did not immediately gather in public squares to vent our anger at the terrorists. In other countries, people would instantly have been on the streets calling for blood. But make no mistake: The anger is there. I just hope that we won't overreact.

—**Andrei Codrescu**, author of *The Devil Never Sleeps, and Other Essays*

Under Atlanta skies so weirdly empty of planes it felt like a solar eclipse, our five kids took in the news. "Like if an airplane was going to hit our house, would you just put me to bed and kiss me goodnight and not tell me?" asked nine-year-old Lily. "And then you'd run away?" Flabbergasted, I sat on her bed to hear more. Turns out she had watched, forbidden, *Titanic* at a friend's house two years ago and felt she recalled a scene in which a mother put her children to bed and then ran for the lifeboats. I corrected her impressions about that fictional mother ("That's why you're not supposed to see movies you're not supposed to see") and reassured her about my own loyalty to her in case of disaster. Two years she carried that fear inside?

Thirteen-year-old Lee worried most about his Pakistani Muslim friend. When the soft-spoken, studious boy became the target of taunts at middle school, a third pal, a Methodist minister's son, punched the assailant in the face, and Lee was proud. These friends, along with a Korean American pal, played Putt-Putt together and went bowling in the week after the attack, and talked nonstop about baseball.

Our 17-year-old trombone-playing son, a week into ownership of his first car (used, and aquamarine) was the most inscrutable. He said little about terrorism but pored over newspapers in private. He did look up once to ask, "Is there a draft?"

Our 19-year-old college daughter awoke to fear and despair; she couldn't reach her friend at NYU by E-mail or cell phone. A couple of days passed before she got an E-mail from him in his temporary quarters. He'd seen everything. He was shattered. Now our daughter is helping to circulate peace petitions, a fine old Oberlin College tradition.

"The bad man told a plane to fly into a building?" cried six-year-old Jesse. "THAT is a VERY bad idea."

"Jackie Chan can help America!" he enthused that night. He'd thought he overheard the word "China" on TV. "Jackie Chan will catch the bad man."

"I don't want to be Gypsy or Jewish anymore," he announced the next day. (He was adopted two years ago from Bulgaria.) "I want to be Chinese."

"No," I said, "but you can help Jackie Chan when you grow up." Pleased by this, he began trying to get in shape by ambushing his brothers and kicking them. "When I help Jackie Chan, I'll live in China?" he asked worriedly.

"No," I said, "you'll still live at home."

"Sleep, then fight with Jackie Chan, then sleep?" he asked.

"Yes."

"Is Jackie Chan real?" he asked on the third day.

"Yes."

"Can ANYBODY beat Jackie Chan?"

"No."

By the fourth day he was asking, "Why does Jackie Chan like me so much?"

Thoughts of love lost, war, middle school bullies, abandonment, and the bad man: Every secret nightmare was released from under every child's bed, from every child's closet, when the nation's invulnerability faltered.

—**Melissa Fay Greene**, author of *The Temple Bombing*

Even though the attack came on a clear morning, I get scared at night. In a history class during my sophomore year of college, I remember learning that the English curfew was adopted by our American colonies almost as soon as we began to settle as a nation. Apparently a curfew was one habit worth importing. My scratchy handwriting copied down the professor's lecture as follows: "Around 1650, a man would be

Preston Keres/U.S. Navy

hired to ring a bell at nine o'clock in the evening and at five in the morning. Between these hours all fires had to be covered (curfew—from the French *couvrir feu*) to avoid danger to the community." It's been more than 20 years since I made those notes, but the fact stays with me.

Why did this definition of "curfew" leap to mind on September 11; why did I search for those notes? Because on that Tuesday I felt (more than felt—knew, understood, conceived) the thousand dark, cold nights driving people throughout time to gather in clusters around fires. Even with the threat of fire's destruction, people drew together in order to keep out the darkness. I recognized the collective fear of night's chaos in my bones. In my bones I also believed, against all reason, that if life were wound up properly (be good, act fairly), safety could be chimed in at evening and at dawn. It sounded like a good idea to me. Cover the fires; hire a watchman.

Draw shutters against the night. Even the familiar becomes dangerous when you can't see it. In the dark you can break your neck scrambling through your own room.

Accidents and acts of terrorism remind us of how precarious life really is—and sudden death, death in an instant, is the scariest of all. September 11 terrified us because it made us realize our fragility as individuals, not only our vulnerability as a country. It made the whole world into a dark room where we cannot help but stumble.

And there are still tricky emotional moments on even calm, clear mornings because when I'm not feeling scared, I'm feeling guilty.

Sometimes it doesn't feel okay to feel okay. It can feel odd to feel good—or to feel even simply ordinary. It's the sort of somersault of the heart that can make you want to slap your own hand when you find yourself thinking of what's for supper instead of how to make the world more peaceful. It's the same impulse that stops you from running up with a big smile and throwing your arms around a favorite relative at a funeral. It's the "How Dare You?" catch, the "Have You Forgotten What Happened?" warning light.

We're in the middle of having to recalibrate our responses of fear, relief, worry and happiness in these weeks after the attack. We're in the middle of learning not to take either the most ordinary day or night for granted.

—**Regina Barreca**, author of *Sweet Revenge: The Wicked Delights of Getting Even*

I was never in any danger, and for that I almost felt guilty. But, yes, I was in New York City the morning of September 11, 2001—sitting in the Green Room of the NBC studios, minutes away from being interviewed by Al Roker of the *Today* show concerning the new edition of *The Old Farmer's Almanac.*

Suddenly, I never in my life felt so irrelevant.

Four or five hours later, after finally being able to reach home and my office in Dublin, N.H., by telephone, I found myself wandering along Fifth Avenue. The billowing black smoke to the south was horrendous, and the streets were practically empty of traffic. Here and there in front of certain windows, groups of people were gathered together, watching television sets inside. Everyone was talking with each other, commiserating with each other, as if we were all old friends.

At some point, I heard and then saw four policemen on motorcycles escorting no fewer than six trailer trucks, all marked as carrying medical supplies, barreling down the avenue, through red lights, toward the smoke. I felt a lump in my throat. While we were all quietly wandering about in the September sunshine, chatting away with each other, they were heading for a hell on earth. The lump in my throat just would not go away that afternoon.

— **Judson D. Hale Sr.**, Editor in Chief, *Yankee*

AFP/Corbis

from the mayor. And the just-turned-four-year-old little sister listened to the news reports and shook her head, and waxed indignant, and said, "They should have been more careful. They should have watched where they were going, the men driving the airplanes. They shouldn't have hit the buildings. They should have been more careful."

And her big sister corrected her, as big sisters do, and in the process showed me the yardstick. "They were watching where they were going," she said. "They wanted to hit the buildings. It wasn't an accident."

"Yes it was!"

"No. It wasn't." Not mad. Not bossy. Just quiet.

I was glad I was driving, and facing forward, and couldn't see what the huge hazel eyes looked like as she spoke. I was glad she couldn't see mine either. Because at that moment I discovered one of the things that must happen sometime between just-turned-four and almost-seven. Something must happen that permits them to entertain the possibility of a world that is not gentle, not designed just to delight them; a world that has twists and caves and wounds laced through it, where evil has room to grow. Little sister protested: She could not entertain the possibility. Big sister explained: somehow she had come to know differently.

You learn everything about children by listening to them explain the world to each other. It was also big sister who explained that yes, Mommy was going to die someday, so was Daddy, so was everyone they loved, but that we would become angels. And watch over and protect them. I don't know at what point she had discovered that the world could be wicked, but sometime she had also discovered it could be sublime.

September 11 left every parent with new tools, even as it tore down so many of the comfortable structures we've lived in for so long. When we talk about courage now, we have stories to tell of firefighters who ran toward the flames, and volunteers who ran to help in a rescue, and a city that became a sanctuary, an island of candles and ashes, and leaders who called on citizens to remember and count the blessings they had taken for granted, and work to defend them in whatever way they could.

In the days to come we would have to explain about fighting, and about when and why people kill other people. We explain the heroism of soldiers and the stern sorrow of war and the price people through history have paid to achieve peace. And the yardstick has a few more notches, and our children are growing up faster than we wanted. But for that matter, so are we all.

—Nancy Gibbs, Senior Editor, *Time*

W e all have our favorite ways of measuring our kids. A pencil mark on the kitchen door. The pants that get suddenly too short. The favorite book they can finally read for themselves. But September 11 introduced a new system of measurement into our house: a yardstick marked off in innocence and discovery and recognition, of what the world contained.

I discovered this where moms discover everything that matters in their children's lives: in the car. My daughters were in the backseat, one who had just turned four three days before the attacks, and her big six-almost-seven-year-old sister. The radio was on, even the giddy music stations were confused, do we escape into a more peaceful time, shanananana, doo-wop doo-wop, or interrupt with the latest update from downtown: the most recent body count; a funeral for a fireman; a message

On that morning of mornings of our young century, I was in global terms as far from cherished New York as it was possible to be. I was at midnight, and beyond the window of a lodge we were staying in amidst the mountains eight hours drive from Sydney, a rare spring blizzard was battering the red gum trees peculiar to the oldest fragment of Gondwana, Australia. Midnight our time, a rage of wind on ancient hills and plains, screaming towards the lustrous coastline. An entire ocean, and then a continent, lay between threatened New York friends and us. But the geographic measures meant nothing. Fear for innumerable friends came instantly—for my publisher, Nan Talese, and her husband, Gay. For Amanda Urban at ICM. My old speech agent, tough girl, Carole Bruckner. Academics at NYU. An Australian treasure, the great novelist Peter Carey, who lives in the Village. Relatives whose grandparents, my forebears' siblings, caught the shorter boat to New York instead of taking the long transglobal swing to Australia. And so on and so on. I wouldn't have much access to E-mail, or the phone, though, till I got home.

The other people in the lodge knew New York too. I don't believe New Yorkers realize the extent to which the world sees their city as everyone's city. Had a New Yorker been present, I like to believe he or she would have been comforted by the intimacy of our outrage. By now, on the TV set in the lounge, we saw the second, banking, ruthlessly directed plane go in. We might have been at the outer limit of the world's shrieks, but we were one in a fraternity of outrage. As we watched, a huge fog had come down on our mountain, as if to enclose us in New York's dusty tragedy—though as friends later told me, it was not only a matter of dusty murk, but of a smell sweeping uptown on the wind, needling into the core of the soul, and unsettling all propositions of normality.

Enclosed in that Australian mist, and disbelieving and exclaiming and speculating, we, a small group of middle-aged Australians, had all the debates which in later days would surface on editorial pages and in op-ed pieces. But one thing astonished me and confirmed my admiration for the abiding better angels of America. I happened by utter accident to have on the trip a brilliant biography, Allen C. Guelzos's *Abraham Lincoln: Redeemer President,* a lucid examination of the intellectual roots of Lincoln's remarkable soul and graphic oratory. I was astonished and delighted now to see, after all the circuses over hanging and pregnant chads, that the same wellsprings began to flow. The august and enduring founding rhetoric, and sense of salutary ritual, swung into place, and dignity and bravery seemed dominant, and gracious imagery seemed to awaken on everyone's lips. Our Australian wryness and gift for the laconic has always teased this aspect of America, and sometimes mocked it, but there was no doubting the authentic product now. A sense that America and the rest of us—for there were a quotient of Australians offered up in that awful hecatomb too—was consoled, united in fraternity, lasted for many days, reinforced by the touching speech of George W, a fellow most people here didn't want to see elected President but now felt at least temporarily annealed to.

It's easy for me to say all this, and I feel guilty that it's easy. I certainly can understand those who choose to see the September 11 disaster as a rootless act of malice and inhuman fanaticism. But after the way the last century went, we ought to be careful how we use that word "inhuman." For we know that savagery and ethnic hysteria are all too human—in fact, one of the tragic marks of our nature—and recur with a depressing, almost seasonal regularity. It is the occasional act of grace and heroism which transcends the normal limits of the predictably human. It is nobility of soul in others which in fact surprises us by seeming inhuman or more than human in a positive way. As much as I felt kinship with all my American friends, and my former fellow occupants of the Silk Building on Fourth and Broadway, where I had an apartment for some years; as much as I was outraged by the horror on grounds of culture, kinship and memory and blood, I would not have been human if I did not also think of things I had beheld in Africa—scenes of terror, trauma, human misery, disorientation, involving people whose misery went uninterviewed, unmarked, unintervened-upon.

Be assured that here in the antipodes, at football games and public orations, at operas and gallery openings, your dead and ours were mourned. People knelt solemnly on pavements before the consulate general offices to make their homage and let drop tears of kinship. And it is in this spirit that I write these words. But surely it is not a slight to the unjustly slaughtered, the lambs of New York to whose throats no thief should have had the knife, to say that in the end the only sane world will be a just one, and that a just world is what will redeem these frightful events.

On the day after the attack, a Keneally cousin of mine in the New York area got his shunt out after apparently successful chemotherapy. And death, we all hope, shall have no ultimate dominion.

—**Thomas Keneally**, author of *Schindler's List*

When I sat down, I'd been planning to write about how things have changed in the world order post–September 11. I've been reading books on Islam, consulting obscure publications like *Jane's Defense Weekly,* and getting used to Humvees on every corner. I'm studying all the chemicals that might be poured into the nearby reservoir now guarded by sentries carrying M-16s. I call members of Congress to see what they know. And I clean.

Actually, I clean more than I call. I took the small attachment to the vacuum cleaner, the one not worth the aggravation to use ordinarily, and sucked up every cobweb in my house. Even that nether region under the radiators would now pass the white glove test. This wouldn't be worth mentioning, except there's a lot of this going around. Senator Richard Shelby, vice chairman of the Intelligence Committee, lives on my street and we marveled Tuesday morning about how the street was spilling over with black trash bags. A lot of closets being cleaned out. I told the senator about my own and how I'd blitzed the kitchen cabinets, tossing stale spices and ancient condiments, and then trimmed the ivy around the windows, which I then washed. "There's a lot of nervous energy around. Gives you a sense of control, doesn't it?" he said, climbing into his newly shined car.

Sort of. Seeking order in the midst of chaos is one source of the nervous energy. But what's disturbing a lot of people is a deeper question that rises not from the evil we've seen but from the goodness: Thrown into the same circumstances, would we behave as well as those who performed feats of courage and kindness? Would I risk my own life to help a colleague? A stranger? Would I, like the maintenance worker in the basement of the WTC, leave the relative safety of my office for the 44th floor to help people down?

Here is the other thing about the heroism we saw and read about: These were for the most part the back-office people of the financial world and the Port Authority and government services. The Masters of the Universe work uptown. The moguls who do work in the WTC for the most part don't catch the early train to get in by nine. How people behaved was in many cases inversely proportional to their position in the corporate hierarchy. WTC security guard Esmerlin Salcedo was in no peril on the day of the attack, since he was attending a computer class at a safe distance away. But when he heard of the first strike, he raced from his class to his desk at the command center on the B-1 level. He walked fellow worker Roselyn Braud to an open exit and told her to run for her life. The last time he was seen he was helping another guard to safety. The 36-year-old father of four earned $10.51 an hour. He had an $80,000 life insurance policy.

One of the most depressing stories I heard is of the Famous Gazillionaire Businessman who found himself and his private jet marooned in Europe when all U.S. airports were shut down. He got in touch with Secretary of Transportation Norman Mineta, who personally refused his entreaties. Then the FGB took his request all the way to the President of the United States to get an exemption for his plane on the grounds that as a Famous Gazillionaire Businessman he was critical to the functioning of America. To his eternal credit, when Mineta got the second request from the White House, he refused again. Let's name an airport after him!

But, as I say, the story still depresses me. That one, and a hundred other stories beyond the big ones of buildings brought down and thousands of innocent people killed. I'm hardly alone. The Pew Research Center released a report that said nearly three quarters of Americans felt depressed over the terrorist attacks, and nearly half were having difficulty concentrating and one third were having trouble sleeping—and this survey was taken before anthrax started coming in the mail. Almost 70 percent of Pew's respondents said they were praying. I'm doing some of that, and lots of scrubbing. I discovered yesterday that many others are seeking solace in sugar. At the Safeway last night, there wasn't one pint of Ben & Jerry's left, not even a default flavor, like vanilla. The manager said he'd never seen such a run on ice cream.

—**Margaret Carlson**, Senior Writer, *Time*

It's the awful magnitude of what happened and that it happened here, out of the blue, that is so hard to take, so inexpressibly heartbreaking, so beyond anything in our experience on home ground.

But everything hasn't changed, as some say. Fly to North Carolina or out to Nebraska, or Ohio and Pennsylvania, as I have in the days since, and look down, look at it all, green and immense, bigger even than you remember. Talk to people, and you're reminded how very much that matters is unchanged.

How is it that he still stands so straight and looks so fit and strong, I asked a man at a reception in Omaha who had told me he was past ninety. "What is your secret?" I asked. "I'm a Nebraska farmer," he said.

We are still the freest, strongest, richest, most inventive, productive, generous nation on earth. That is plain truth. Our military is second to none. Our economy, for all its bumps, remains the strongest of any nation's. Our resources are surpassing, and include the most valuable of resources in a fast-changing, dangerous world: brain power.

In many ways I feel prouder about the country now, since September 11, than I have in a long while. We've witnessed some of the most stirring examples of selfless courage and real-life heroism in our lifetime, and a return on all sides of respect for courage and heroism. Genuine love of country is as evident as at almost any time in memory. We're united as we've not been for 50 years or more. Overnight the most divisive Congress in memory has become the most unified.

We've seen the veteran mayor of our greatest city and the new, untried President of the United States rise to the occasion in the tradition of the best who have served in high office. As a people we seem to be both keeping our heads and using our heads.

And to our very great advantage there is one further, inexhaustible source of strength for all to draw on—our history, our story as a free people. As Churchill reminded us in December 1941, when prospects appeared as dark as they had ever been, we have not journeyed all this way because we are made of sugar candy.

"And the commitment of our fathers," said President Bush at the national prayer service, "is now the calling of our time."

Amen.

—**David McCullough**, author of *John Adams*

As sunshine glittered on the surface of the Hudson River, and Ground Zero smoldered across the way, young boys in Hoboken, N.J., returned to their Saturday morning soccer games.

Heinz Kluetmeier for Sports Illustrated

The New Normal

New Yorkers and Washingtonians—indeed, all Americans—returned to their work and play with an altered sensibility. They resumed their daily routines to prove that the terrorists had not won the day, but in "the new normal" they realized that there are many in this world who hate them—hate the United States and all that it stands for. They knew that in the new normal, life was dangerous. And, on October 7, they knew that their country had launched its offensive. America got back to living its life, but throughout the fall, September 11 cast a resolute shadow.

Within a week the stock exchanges were back in business (left, on September 17, Wall Street's reopening). Within two weeks, flags were back at full staff. But things were not the same. The market had been rocked. Companies that had lost offices at the World Trade Center were scrambling for space. And workers elsewhere in the city had to wonder, Are the airports safe? What about Grand Central? How hard would it be to slip anthrax into the air conditioning?

America was bombing Afghanistan and someone was attacking America. A shadow of fear spread as the tabloids, the networks and the Senate were hit by anthrax-laced mail. In New York City's Grand Central Terminal (right), National Guardsmen were a constant presence. More people were taking trains as searches snarled traffic at the tunnels, and some parents who commuted as a couple began to travel separately—so that at least one would survive an attack.

Nina Berman/Aurora for TIME

The national pastime suspended play in the wake of September 11. But as with the nation's business, it felt right to start anew on Monday, and on the 17th the cry rang out, "Play ball!" Never was "The Star-Spangled Banner" sung more fervently than when the reigning world champion New York Yankees surged into postseason play.

Shannon Stapleton

Lorenzo Ciniglio/Corbis Sygma

Les Stone/Sipa

All of them were innocent. Hundreds of them laid down their lives in an effort to save others. Ultimately, slowly, the thought emerged that these people—more than 5,000 in all—were victims of war, civilian casualties in a cruel and dirty conflict. This sentiment was formalized on October 7 when bombs rained on targets throughout Afghanistan, shouting that the wrongfully dead in lower New York City, in Arlington, Va., and in a remote field in western Pennsylvania would not be forgotten.

New York's fallen firemen: Tears were shed at St. Francis of Assisi Friary for chaplain Father Mychal Judge. A fire engine served as hearse at St. Patrick's Cathedral after Lt. Dennis Mojica's funeral.

In Memoriam

We Will Never Forget

One didn't have to be in New York or Washington to pay respects. Tucker Hodgson and his five-month-old daughter, Paytan, paused amid a sea of remembrance in Guthrie, Okla. The Bible Baptist Church there had placed 5,000 crosses in a field, one for each person lost on September 11.

AP

Over There

Jockel Finck/AP

The Arabian Sea, October 11, 2001. An F-18 prepared for takeoff from the flight deck of the USS *Enterprise*, one of the ships participating in Operation Enduring Freedom.

3
S

Rajesh Mirpuri
2nd Floor, left
105th Floor WTC parking
Tower 1

Joe Visciano
DOB 2/25/79   Please Call
(718) 966-3576

Lizie McNiver-Cole
9.25.68 SS
Hight 5-2
1212
TEL. 790.9728

MISSING
PAUL ORTIZ JR.

Paul Ortiz Jr. has been missing since yesterday. The last time he was heard from is yesterday (Sept. 11, 2001) at about 9:30am He was at the Windows of the World restaurant. He hasn't been heard from since. He works for Bloomberg.

Any information regarding Paul Ortiz Jr. should be relayed to his family. Please contact us at the following numbers:

Star Ortiz (wife)
Paul Ortiz (father)
Sophie Ortiz (mother)

MISSING

DEBORAH KAPLAN
(201) 634-9297
OR
(631) 368-0180
BRUCE

PAUL CURIOLI
17 TANGLEWOOD LANE
NORWALK, CT 06851 1-203-838-7084

6'1   170lb   BROWN HAIR, BROWN EYES,
MUSTACHE

51 YEARS OLD, NO TATOO'S, GOLD WEDDING
RING
WEARING DARK SUIT, WHITE SHIRT AND TIE

WORKS FOR: F M GLOBAL NORWALK, CT
WAS AT MEETING FOR AON BUSSINESS WITH
PFIZER AT TOWER 2 102 FLOOR

ANY INFORMATION PLEASE ABOVE NUMBER
A.S.A.P.

We're trying to get
information on
**Abe
Zelmanowitz**
(known to some
as Avremel).

He works for Empire Blue Cross/Blue Shield
at 1 World Trade Center, on the 27th floor.
Approx 5'8", average build, greyish hair, age 55, trimmed beard, glasses

When he called us at about 9:30am to say he was ok,
the evacuation had already begun,
but he was staying with a co-worker, Edward (Ed) Beyea,
who's a quadriplegic. That was after the original explosion,
but before the building collapsed.

We can be reached at 718/677-8699
or 718/951-3722 or 917/374-7640
Mr. and Mrs. Zelmanowitz • Mr. and Mrs. Stern

Thanks for your efforts.

MISSING
LORISA TAYLOR

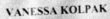

of MARSH & McLENNON
PRIVATE CLIENT SERVICES
1 WORLD TRADE CENTER
94TH FLOOR

Age: 31
Height: 5'8" Weight: 147 lbs
Black Female (medium complexion)
Hair: Dark Brown (Shoulder length)
Wearing Navy Blue suit with light blue blouse

If you have any information, please call:
718 859 1092   718 859 5402
917 673 0630   800 581 8771

If you are looking for someone from Marsh, please call. Perhaps we can work together to find our family and friends.

VANESSA KOLPAK

Ht: 5'3"   Hair: Blonde
Eyes: blue/green   Weight: 130 lbs.
Phone: 212-561-1978 or 312-608-0051

Missing
Name:
Address:
Phone:
Contact:
S.S.#:
Dentist:
Doctor:
Scars:
Birthday:
Company:
Location:
Next of
Contact:

Person

Edward Stark
917 539 0147